ATLAS
Grade 3 English Practice

GET DIGITAL ACCESS TO

2 ATLAS Practice Tests

Personalized Study Plans

REGISTER NOW

Important Instruction

Register online using the link and the access code provided by your teacher.

Enter the access code (for your reference) in the box given below.

Access Code:

ATLAS Online Assessments and Grade 3 English Language Arts Literacy (ELA) Practice Workbook, Student Copy

Contributing Author - Leigh Hargett
Contributing Author - Anneda Nettleton
Contributing Author - George Smith
Contributing Author - Wendy Bundgaard
Executive Producer - Mukunda Krishnaswamy
Program Director - Anirudh Agarwal
Designer and Illustrator - Sowmya R.

ISBN 13: 979-8859879250

Printed in the United States of America

CONTACT INFORMATION

LUMOS INFORMATION SERVICES, LLC

 PO Box 1575, Piscataway, NJ 08855-1575
www.LumosLearning.com

 Email: support@lumoslearning.com
Tel: (732) 384-0146
Fax: (866) 283-6471

Lumos Learning
Step Up Your Skills

INTRODUCTION

This book is specifically designed to improve student achievement on the Arkansas Teaching and Learning Assessment System(ATLAS). Students perform at their best on standardized tests when they feel comfortable with the test content as well as the test format. Lumos online practice tests are meticulously designed to mirror the state assessment. They adhere to the guidelines provided by the state for the number of sessions and questions, standards, difficulty level, question types, test duration and more.

Based on our decade of experience developing practice resources for standardized tests, we've created a dynamic system, the Lumos Smart Test Prep Methodology. It provides students with realistic assessment rehearsal and an efficient pathway to overcoming each proficiency gap.

Use the Lumos Smart Test Prep Methodology to achieve a high score on the ATLAS.

Lumos Smart Test Prep Methodology

1 The student takes the first online diagnostic test, which assesses proficiency levels in various standards.

2 StepUp generates a personalized online study plan based on the student's performance.

3 The student completes targeted practice in the printed workbook and marks it as complete in the online study plan.

4 The student then attempts the second online practice test.

5 StepUp generates a second individualized online study plan.

6 The student completes the targeted practice and is ready for the actual ATLAS.

Table of Contents

Chapter 1 - Reading Literature

Lesson 1: The Question Session

Question 1-3 are based on the story below

After reading the story, enter the details in the map below. This will help you to answer the questions that follow.

Margaret was a simple lady who lived in a village with her husband, Robert. They had a daughter named Amy. Every day at sunrise, Margaret would wake up, cook, clean, and feed the cattle. Robert would milk the cows and then take the dogs for a long walk. Amy would study, help her mother for some time, and then get ready for school.

Amy studied in a school that was far away from her house, but she loved going to school. She went with her friends, Ingrid and Rebecca. They would walk together chatting, laughing, and singing songs as they went. They had to cross a river on the way. The only way they could cross it was by walking on a narrow bridge.

One day Margaret, Robert, Amy, and her friends were walking on the narrow bridge one behind the other. Amy and her friends were off to school, as usual, Margaret and Robert wanted to go to the market on the other side of the river to buy groceries for the house.

As they were crossing the narrow bridge, Rebecca slipped. She gave a frightened scream, clutching Ingrid, who was in front of her. Both of them lost their balance and fell into the river. Amy clutched her mother in fright. For a moment, she hesitated and then threw herself into the river after her friends, determined to save them.

Margaret screamed, and Robert jumped into the river. Some passers-by also jumped into the river and rescued the children, who were dripping wet, and shivering with fright.

That night Robert patted his daughter Amy and said, "You are a brave girl Amy, I'm proud of you."

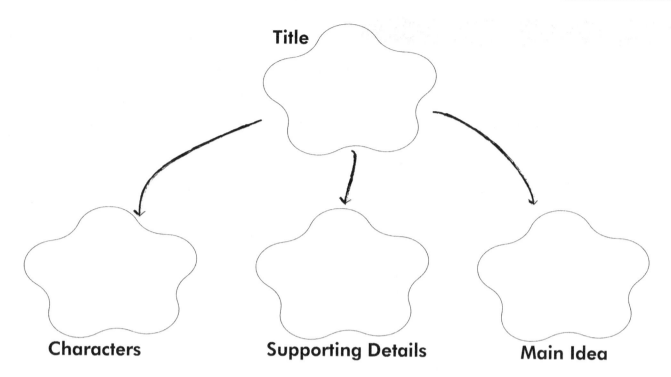

1. How is Margaret related to Amy?

- Ⓐ She is her cousin.
- Ⓑ She is her friend.
- Ⓒ She is her mother.
- Ⓓ She is her aunt.

2. Who slipped on the narrow bridge?

- Ⓐ Amy
- Ⓑ Margaret
- Ⓒ Robert
- Ⓓ Rebecca

3. Why did Robert and Margaret go along with the girls?

- Ⓐ They wanted to walk them to school.
- Ⓑ They wanted to go for a walk.
- Ⓒ They wanted to buy some groceries.
- Ⓓ They wanted to walk on the bridge.

Question 4 is based on the story below

After reading the story, enter the details in the map below. This will help you to answer the questions that follow.

One day, a baby elephant was happily dancing through the jungle, nodding his head and lifting up his trunk to trumpet loudly.

The loud sound woke up a monkey who was sleeping in a tree nearby. He was very angry. He scolded the elephant and asked him to keep quiet.

"You silly animal," he said. "Can't you keep quiet? I'm sleeping."

"Oh, sorry," said the little elephant and walked on. After sometime, the little elephant reached a river and saw some beautiful swans there. He gazed at the beautiful birds. The swans looked at him and began to laugh.

"Oh! Look at that big creature," they said. "What a long nose, his ears are like fans, and look at his skin, it's much too big for him. He looks like a big wrinkled bag with all those folds!" They laughed at him and swam away.

The little elephant was very sad. He tried to smooth out his skin with his trunk but it was no good. He thought, "Why am I so ugly? Let me hide so that no one can see me."

He tried to hide himself in a thick bush but he disturbed some nests. The birds flew above his head crying loudly and tried to peck him.

Suddenly, he saw a big bear coming towards him. It was growling and appeared to be very angry. The little elephant was very frightened, and he trumpeted loudly. Just as he trumpeted, he heard a loud crashing and stomping. A herd of wrinkled elephants came charging to the rescue.

Seeing the herd, the frightened bear ran away.

The little elephant joyfully ran to the big elephants, thanked them, and said, "I wish I could be like you. You're so mighty and strong," he continued.

"But you are," replied the elephants. "You're a perfect little elephant." The little elephant danced for joy; he trumpeted loudly and walked away happily with the other elephants following behind.

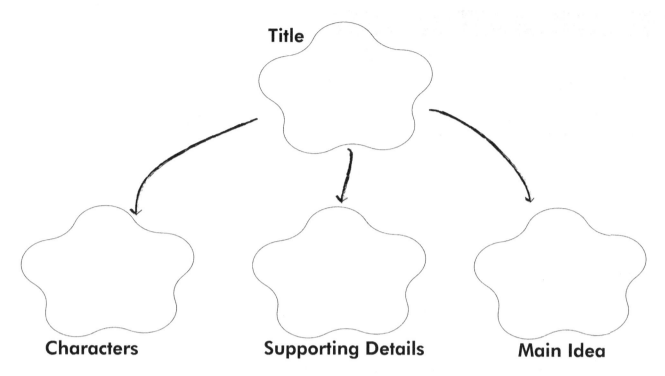

Title

Characters   **Supporting Details**   **Main Idea**

4. According to the story, why does an elephant's skin look 'wrinkly'?

   (A) It is grey in color.
   (B) It has too many folds.
   (C) It is thick.
   (D) It is hard.

Camels are bumpy,
Their backs are all lumpy,
Giraffes are long- legged and meek:
Bears are so growly,
Hyenas are howly,
Dolphins are slippery and sleek.

Kangaroos have a pocket,
But no way to lock it,
Their babies can look out and peep,
But monkeys are funny,
I wish I had money,
Enough to buy one and keep.

5. According to the poem, where is the camel's hump?

   Ⓐ on its stomach
   Ⓑ on its back
   Ⓒ underneath its stomach
   Ⓓ it has no hump

6. According to the poem, which animal is long-legged?

   Ⓐ Hyena
   Ⓑ Camel
   Ⓒ Giraffe
   Ⓓ Elephant

7. Part A

What does the poem say about Dolphin?

7. Part B

What does the poem say causes dolphins to be slippery?

8. **Read the Poem. Match each animal to its characteristic, put a tick mark against the characteristic for each animal.**

Animals	Has Hump	Has Pocket	Slippery	Long legged
Kangaroo				
Camel				
Giraffe				
Dolphins				

Question 9 is based on the story below

After reading the story, enter the details in the map below. This will help you to answer the questions that follow.

Once upon a time, there was a wealthy woman that had very poor eyesight. She decided to call a doctor to ask if he could restore her eyesight. The doctor promised to cure her but told her that she had to pay him a huge fee. He also told her that throughout the treatment she had to keep her eyes closed. The woman agreed to both requirements.

The doctor began the treatment in the woman's home. Every day the doctor stole something from the lady's house. The treatment lasted a lengthy period of time. Finally, when he had emptied her house, the doctor told her that he had finished her treatment, and that her eyesight was restored.

The woman was very happy that the treatment was over, but she refused to pay the doctor. The doctor was very angry that she refused to pay his hefty fee. He told her that he was taking her to court. She just laughed at him.

When the judge asked the woman to explain why she didn't pay the doctor, the woman said, "Sir, before the operation, I was partially blind, but at least I could see the things in my home." She continued, "But now after the treatment, I am unable to see anything in my home. The woman solemnly told the judge, I must be totally blind because I can see nothing."

The judge looked at the doctor, who hung his head in shame. The doctor realized that the woman knew that he had stolen all her things. He felt ashamed and returned everything he had stolen. The doctor also said that the woman did not owe him a fee for the treatment.

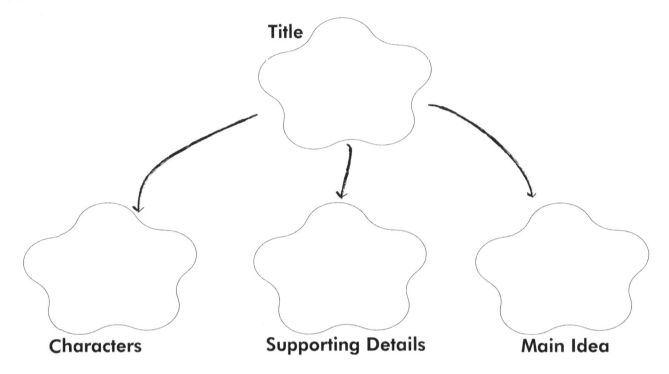

9. **What was the old lady's eye sight like before her operation?**

   Ⓐ   She was not able to see anything.
   Ⓑ   She could only see one thing.
   Ⓒ   She could see things but not very clearly.
   Ⓓ   She was totally blind.

Question 10 is based on the story below

After reading the story, enter the details in the map below. This will help you to answer the questions that follow.

Brandon lived with his mother at one end of the forest. His school was at the other end of the forest. Every day he had to go through the forest to get to school and the forest was very scary.

One day he told his mother that he felt very scared to cross that forest.

His mother said, "Don't be scared" "Your brother lives in the forest. Whenever you get scared, you can always call him. He won't answer you but he will see that no harm comes to you."

Brandon said, "Why didn't you tell me about my brother earlier? What is his name?"

Mother said, "His name is Courage. Whenever you get frightened, call his name, and he will silently follow you to school and see that you come back home safely."

The next day Brandon was happy to get ready for school. He was not scared as he went through the forest on the way to school. That day, while coming home from school, he got scared when he heard the sounds of animals. Then he remembered his mother's words remembering him that his brother would protect him whenever he was frightened.

Brandon called out "Courage, Courage" with full confidence. Suddenly he began to feel better. He began to feel brave. He again called out, "Courage!, Courage!" He thought that his brother was silently following him, he began to sing softly and then loudly. He realized that he was not frightened after all. He crossed the forest confidently with courage.

The only traits we need to have to move ahead are confidence and courage in ourselves.

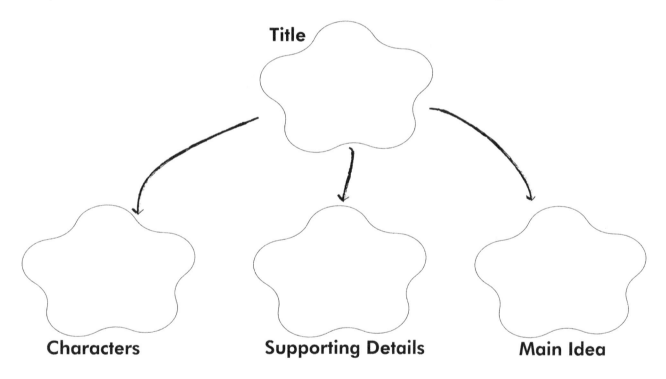

10. What is the best title for this story?

After reading the story, enter the details in the map below. This will help you to answer the questions that follow.

Eight-year-old Tess heard her parents talking about her little brother Andrew. She realized something was wrong. Andrew was very sick, and they did not have enough money for his treatment. Tess heard her daddy say, "Only a miracle can save him now."

Tess went to her bedroom and retrieved a jar from its hiding place. There were a few coins in it. She counted them carefully. She then made her way to the drug store. The pharmacist was too busy to pay attention to her. "And what do you want?" he asked, annoyed at her persistence. "Can't you see that I am talking to my brother? He is here from Chicago."

Tess persisted, "My brother's really sick …….. and I want to buy a miracle. His name is Andrew. He has something bad growing inside of his head and my daddy says only a miracle can save him now. So, how much does a miracle cost?" Tess rambled.

The pharmacist's brother, a well-dressed man, stooped down and asked the girl. "What kind of miracle does your brother need?"

"Don't know," replied Tess, eyes welling up with tears. "I just know Mommy says he needs an operation. But my daddy can't pay for it. So, I want to use my money."

The man from Chicago asked, "How much money do you have?"

"One dollar and eleven cents," said Tess.

"Well, what a coincidence," smiled the man.

"One dollar and eleven cents is the exact price of a miracle for your little brother." He took her money in one hand and grasped Tess's hand in the other. "Take me to where you live. I want to see your brother and meet your parents. Let's see if I have the kind of miracle you need."

The well-dressed man was Carlton Armstrong, a neurosurgeon. He operated on Andrew without charging any money. It wasn't long until Andrew was home and well again. "I wonder how much the surgery cost?" said Mother.

Tess smiled to herself. She knew exactly how much the miracle cost— one dollar and eleven cents…. plus the immense faith of a little child.

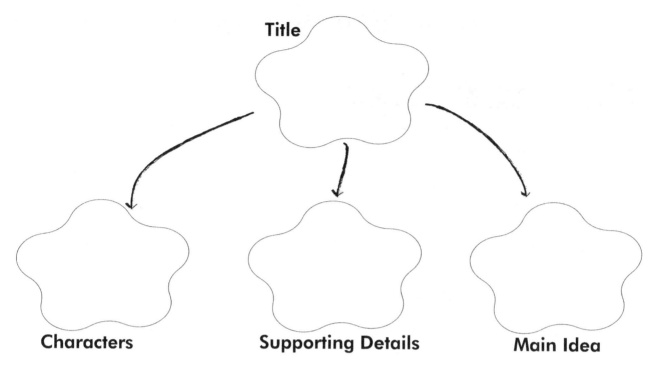

Title

Characters   **Supporting Details**   **Main Idea**

11. Who saved Andrew in this story?

12. Why were Tess's parents worried? Circle the correct answer choice.

- Ⓐ They did not know what was wrong with her brother.
- Ⓑ Tess had little money in her piggybank.
- Ⓒ Andrew was sick and they had no money for treatment.
- Ⓓ Tess did not know the price of a miracle.

CHAPTER 1 → Lesson 2: Tell Me Again

Question 1-3 are based on the story below

After reading the story, enter the details in the map below. This will help you to answer the questions that follow.

One day, a baby elephant was happily dancing through the jungle, nodding his head and lifting his trunk to trumpet loudly.

The loud sound woke up a monkey who was sleeping in a tree nearby. He was very angry. He scolded the elephant and asked him to keep quiet.

"You silly animal," he said. "Can't you keep quiet? I'm sleeping."

"Oh, sorry," said the little elephant, and walked on. After some time, the little elephant reached a river and saw some beautiful swans there. He gazed at the beautiful birds. The swans looked at him and began to laugh.

"Oh! Look at that big creature," they said. "What a long nose, his ears are like fans, and look at his skin, it's much too big for him. He looks like a big wrinkled bag with all of those folds!" They laughed at him and swam away.

The little elephant was very sad. He tried to smooth out his skin with his trunk, but it was no good. He thought, "Why am I so ugly? Let me hide so that no one can see me."

He tried to hide in a thick bush, but he disturbed some nests. The birds flew above his head, crying loudly while trying to peck at him.

The little elephant ran for cover. He went behind a big rock to hide. Suddenly, he saw a big bear coming towards him. It was growling and appeared to be very angry. The little elephant was very frightened and trumpeted loudly. Just as he trumpeted, he heard a loud crashing and stomping. A herd of elephants came charging to the rescue.

Seeing the herd, the frightened bear ran away.

The little elephant joyfully ran to the big elephants, thanked them, and said, "I wish I could be like you. You're so mighty and strong," he continued.

"But you are," replied the elephants. "You're a perfect little elephant." The little elephant danced for joy; he trumpeted loudly and walked away happily with the other elephants following behind.

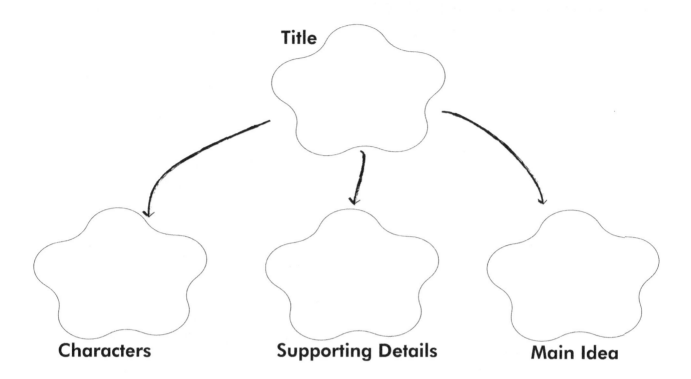

1. What caused the monkey to wake up in this story?

Ⓐ   The wind was making a loud noise.
Ⓑ   The elephant trumpeted loudly.
Ⓒ   The monkey fell down.
Ⓓ   The monkey was not asleep in the story.

2. Why did the swans laugh at the elephant?

Ⓐ   They thought that the elephant looked ugly.
Ⓑ   The elephant was happy.
Ⓒ   The elephant was looking at them.
Ⓓ   The elephant was dancing.

3. In this story, what caused the bear to run away?

Ⓐ   He didn't want to see the monkey.
Ⓑ   He was tired.
Ⓒ   He was frightened by the herd of elephants.
Ⓓ   He wanted to bring its friends.

After reading the story, enter the details in the map below. This will help you to answer the questions that follow.

Brandon lived with his mother at one end of the forest. His school was at the other end of the forest. Every day he had to go through the forest to get to school and the forest was very scary.

One day he told his mother that he felt very scared to cross that forest.

His mother said, "Don't be scared" "Your brother lives in the forest. Whenever you get scared, you can always call him. He won't answer you but he will see that no harm comes to you."

Brandon said, "Why didn't you tell me about my brother earlier? What is his name?"

Mother said, "His name is Courage. Whenever you get frightened, call his name, and he will silently follow you to school and see that you come back home safely."

The next day Brandon was happy to get ready for school. He was not scared as he went through the forest on the way to school. That day, while coming home from school, he got scared when he heard the sounds of animals. Then he remembered his mother's words remembering him that his brother would protect him whenever he was frightened.

Brandon called out "Courage, Courage" with full confidence. Suddenly he began to feel better. He began to feel brave. He again called out, "Courage!, Courage!" He thought that his brother was silently following him, he began to sing softly and then loudly. He realized that he was not frightened after all. He crossed the forest confidently with courage.

The only traits we need to have to move ahead are confidence and courage in ourselves.

4. Who does Brandon's mother tell him lives in the forest?

   Ⓐ   A monster
   Ⓑ   His father
   Ⓒ   His brother
   Ⓓ   Fear

Question 5 is based on the poem below

I quarreled with my brother
I don't know what about,
One thing led to another
And somehow we fell out.
The start of it was slight,
The end of it was strong,
He said he was right,
I knew he was wrong!

We hated one another.
The afternoon turned black.
Then suddenly my brother
Thumped me on the back,
And said, "Oh, come along!
We can't go on all night
I was in the wrong."
So he was in the right.

-by Eleanor Farjeon

5. Who is quarreling in the above poem?

   Ⓐ   The author with her brother.
   Ⓑ   The readers with their brothers.
   Ⓒ   The author with her mother.
   Ⓓ   None of these

Margaret was a simple lady who lived in a village with her husband, Robert. They had a daughter named Amy. Every day at sunrise, Margaret would wake up, cook, clean, and feed the cattle. Robert would milk the cows and then take the dogs for a long walk. Amy would study, help her mother for some time, and then get ready for school.

Amy studied in a school which was far away from her house, but she loved going to school. She went with her friends, Ingrid and Rebecca. They would walk together chatting, laughing, and singing songs as they went. They had to cross a river on the way. The only way they could cross it was by walking on a narrow bridge.

One day Margaret, Robert, and Amy, and her friends were walking on the narrow bridge one behind the other. Amy and her friends were off to school as usual, and Margaret and Robert wanted to go to the market on the other side of the river to buy groceries for the house.

As they were crossing the narrow bridge, Rebecca slipped. She gave a frightened scream, clutching Ingrid, who was in front of her. Both of them lost their balance and fell into the river. Amy clutched her mother in fright. For a moment she hesitated and then threw herself into the river after her friends, determined to save them.

Margaret screamed, and Robert jumped into the river. Some passers-by also jumped into the river and rescued the children, who were dripping wet and shivering with fright.

That night Robert patted his daughter Amy and said, "You are a brave girl Amy, I'm proud of you."

6. According to the story, what did Robert do every morning?

Ⓐ Milk the cows.
Ⓑ Fetch milk from the shop.
Ⓒ Boil the milk.
Ⓓ Take the milk to sell at the market.

7. What did the girls have to cross on their way to school?

Ⓐ A narrow bridge.
Ⓑ A small stream.
Ⓒ A mango grove.
Ⓓ A big field.

After reading the story, enter the details in the map below. This will help you to answer the questions that follow.

Tryouts for Madison

"I have to make the team," Madison said. Madison had thought of nothing but tryouts since the poster was displayed in the hall. She was new to the school. She understood that the other girls had an advantage, but what she lacked in experience, she made up for in effort and attitude. Being on the team would help her make new friends and feel like a part of a group.

The coach told her at the first practice to stretch daily, work on motions, and practice her jumps. This would develop flexibility. She wouldn't be as nervous if she could gain some height on her toe touches. She wanted her coach to know that she would be dedicated and work hard if she was on the team. Madison didn't mind-stretching. She actually found herself doing this while watching television, before and after meals, and before bedtime. While looking in a mirror, she would practice motions. The great thing about stretching and motion practice was that the hot temperatures would not be a factor in stopping her. She could do all the necessary moves in the comforts of air conditioning. Madison's parents could see her determination by the way she stretched and jumped numerous times a day.

Over the next two weeks, as summer faded into fall, Madison continued attending practices, stretching, and jumping. She was focused on being the best cheerleader at tryouts that she could be. She noticed that she was becoming as flexible as a straw. Her jumps were higher and her motions were nice and stiff.

At last, tryout day arrived! Madison quickly dressed in her tryout clothes and set off for the gym. She was smiling and whistling as she made her way to the gym. She had worked hard and practiced every day. Madison thought, "I hope that I do my best and that tryouts are fantastic!"

8. Why was Madison whistling when she entered the gym?

- Ⓐ She made the team.
- Ⓑ She felt good about her chances of making the team.
- Ⓒ She whistles all the time.
- Ⓓ She learned that everyone gets to be on the team.

9. Which character traits best describe Madison?

- Ⓐ unfocused and compassionate
- Ⓑ lazy and uncaring
- Ⓒ brave and loyal
- Ⓓ optimistic and hardworking

10. During which season of the year did the tryouts occur?

- Ⓐ winter
- Ⓑ fall
- Ⓒ spring
- Ⓓ summer

Question 11 is based on the story below

Maggie's Dilemma?

Maggie has many things to accomplish over the weekend. She wants to go to a friend's house for a party on Sunday afternoon. If she doesn't get her chores and homework done, she is afraid that her parents will not let her attend the party.

As she is getting ready for bed, Friday night, she is worrying and wondering how she can do everything before the party on Sunday. Her mother tells her that she needs to prioritize her life. Maggie is not sure what that means. She thinks to herself, "What is prioritize? How does that help me in my life?"

Her older brother, Ronny, comes into her room. He asks her, "Hey, Sis, why the puzzled look? Why are you just sitting there on your bed looking around your room?"

"Ronny, what does it mean when Mom tells me I need to prioritize my life?"
"What's wrong with my life?"

Ron laughs and tells her that she has a tendency to try to do too much stuff in too little time. He suggests that she make a list of what she needs to do. Then, she needs to make a list of what she wants to do. Again, Maggie looks confused.

He takes out one of her notebooks and starts to write. She watches as he puts his name at the top of the list along with the words - Have to Do. Then he makes numbers going down each side. He writes, clean room as number 1. For number 2, he puts down take out the trash. Ron then writes down, mow the yard for number 3.

On another sheet of paper, he does the same thing, only this time after his name, he writes- Want to Do. On the second list, the number 1 is watch wrestling on TV. Number 2 is play video games.

Suddenly, Maggie gets it! "Oh, I see now. Prioritize means to put things in order of importance."

Her brother replies, "Duh, I knew I could help out!" Ron laughs along with Maggie. She is no longer puzzled and starts to write.

11. **Order the story by sequence of events that occurred. Select from the events given below and write in the order in which they occurred in the blank box given below.**

   A. **Maggie finally understands what she needs to do.**
   B. **Maggie asked her brother to explain what her mom had told her.**
   C. **Maggie didn't know if she could go to the party on Sunday if she didn't get all of her chores done before then.**
   D. **Maggie's brother helps her to understand what prioritizing means.**

Question 12 is based on the story below

Bringing a Bear to School

Tyrone was so happy that his teacher said they were going to have a special celebration for a unit they had been studying on Bears in his class. They had been reading many bear books lately. Some of the books were about real bears and some were books about make-believe bears like Paddington and others. Mr. Clark, his teacher, wanted the students to relate to their own real-life experiences. The students were talking about the celebration during class one day.

Mr. Clark told them they could bring a stuffed bear from home if they wanted to or another stuffed animal for the day of the celebration. The girls were all excited. The boys were laughing and snickering about how dumb that idea was. They were saying only sissies would bring or have a stuffed toy. Tyrone's mouth frowned. He loved his Beary. He had Beary since he was just a tiny baby. Tyrone's grandfather had brought it to his mom on the day Tyrone was born. His grandfather had passed away several years later, and Tyrone held Beary all the time he thought about his grandfather. He even saved his allowance and special birthday money to buy his stuffed bear clothes. When Tyrone joined the soccer team, Beary got a soccer outfit. When he joined t-ball, Beary got a baseball uniform, too. So why were the boys making fun of having a stuffed bear? Tyrone did not understand.

The teacher sent home a note the weekend before the celebration explaining to parents what the next school day (Monday) would be like. Mr. Clark said that the students could bring their own stuffed animal if they chose to do so for a show and tell part of the celebration. They were even having zoo personnel come and share their experiences with the bears at the zoo. There would be Bear shaped cookies and cakes, too! Mr. Clark was also bringing his video of his trip to Russia where he saw many polar bears.

It sounded like so much fun! But, Tyrone was still hesitant on whether or not he should bring Beary to school. He wanted to show him off with his clothes and all. He wanted to tell the story of how his grandfather bought him the bear and how much it means to him still.

When Tyrone got home from school on Friday afternoon, he showed his mom the note from Mr. Clark. He had a puzzled look on his face. His mom said it sounded like the class was going to have a wonderful time on Monday. His sister, LaTasha, started laughing loudly. "Oh, please tell me you are not thinking of taking Beary?" she exclaimed.

"I was, but the other boys would probably make fun of me."

His mom said, "Why would they do that, Tyrone? Don't you think they have stuffed animals, too?"

"Maybe mom, but they would never admit it or bring them to school."

So all weekend long, Tyrone pondered what to do. Right before bedtime on Sunday night, he made his decision. Beary and his outfits were ready to go!

On Monday morning, Tyrone's mom decided she would take him to school herself rather than have him walk or ride the bus. When they arrived at his class, Mr. Clark was greeting all of the classmates. The entire classroom was decorated with bears of all sorts. On the front of Mr. Clark's desk was a beautiful stuffed bear. A sign in front said, "My Buddy!" Tyrone grinned from ear to ear as he joyfully took out Beary, dressed him in his baseball uniform, and put him on his desk. He made his own sign, "My Beary!"

Needless to say it was a great day for Tyrone. Several of the other boys had brought their stuffed animals and stuffed bears, too.

12. Order the story by sequence of events that occurred. Select from the events given below and write in the order in which they occurred in the blank box given below.

    A. Tyrone decided to take Beary to school.
    B. His sister, LaTasha, laughed at him.
    C. Mr. Clark had decorated the room in bears, including his own "Buddy" on his desk.
    D. The girls were excited.
    E. Tyrone had a great day at the celebration.
    F. Mr. Clark was going to have a celebration for the class after their unit on bears.

Question 13 and 14 are based on the story below

OLD-FASHIONED FAIRY TALES
By Juliana Horatia Gatty Ewing

The following fairy tale is separated into 4 parts. Each part has questions that go along with the section, to help the reader have a better understanding of the tale. Also, for the reader, the selection has been numbered. Remember to read the selections more than one time for comprehension purposes.

While reading this fairy tale, keep in mind that it is written in what is called Old English. This means some words are used or spelled differently than the vocabulary we use today. Should you have difficulty with the words, use context clues to help. You may also ask your teacher, or use a dictionary to help you understand the meaning.

GOOD LUCK IS BETTER THAN GOLD.

Part 1

1. There was once upon a time a child who had Good Luck for his godfather.

2. "I am not Fortune," said Good Luck to the parents; "I have no gifts to bestow, but whenever he needs help I will be at hand."

3. "Nothing could be better," said the old couple. They were delighted. But what pleases the father often fails to satisfy the son: moreover, every man thinks that he deserves just a little more than he has got, and does not reckon it to the purpose if his father had less.

4. Many a one would be thankful to have as good reasons for contentment as he who had Good Luck for his godfather.

5. If he fell, Good Luck popped something soft in the way to break his fall; if he fought, Good Luck directed his blows, or tripped up his adversary; if he got into a scrape, Good Luck helped him out of it; and if ever Misfortune met him, Good Luck contrived to hustle her on the pathway till his godson got safely by.

6. In games of hazard the godfather played over his shoulder. In matters of choice he chose for him. And when the lad began to work on his father's farm the farmer began to get rich. For no bird or field-mouse touched a seed that his son had sown, and every plant he planted throve when Good Luck smiled on it.

7. The boy was not fond of work, but when he did go into the fields, Good Luck followed him.

8. "Your christening-day was a blessed day for us all," said the old farmer.

9. "He has never given me so much as a lucky sixpence," muttered Good Luck's godson.

10. "I am not Fortune—I make no presents," said the godfather.

11. When we are discontented, it is oftener to please our neighbours than ourselves. It was because the other boys had said—"Simon, the shoemaker's son, has an alderman for his godfather. He gave him a silver spoon with the Apostle Peter for the handle; but thy godfather is more powerful than any alderman"—that Good Luck's godson complained, "He has never given me so much as a bent sixpence."

Part 2

12. By and by the old farmer died, and his son grew up, and had the largest farm in the country. The other boys grew up also, and as they looked over the farmer's boundary-wall, they would say:

13. "Good-morning, Neighbour. That is certainly a fine farm of yours. Your cattle thrive without loss. Your crops grow in the rain and are reaped with the sunshine. Mischance never comes to your road. What you have worked for you enjoy. Such success would turn the heads of poor folk like us. At the same time, one would think a man need hardly work for his living at all who has Good Luck for his godfather."

14. "That is very true," thought the farmer. "Many a man is prosperous, and reaps what he sows, who had no more than the clerk and the sexton for gossips at his christening."

15. "What is the matter, Godson?" asked Good Luck, who was with him in the field.

16. "I want to be rich," said the farmer.

17. "You will not have to wait long," replied the godfather. "In every field you sow, in every flock you

rear there is increase without abatement. Your wealth is already tenfold greater than your father's."

18. "Aye, aye," replied the farmer. "Good wages for good work. But many a young man has gold at his command who need never turn a sod, and none of the Good People came to his christening. Fortunatus's Purse now, or even a sack or two of gold—"

19. "Peace!" cried the godfather; "I have said that I give no gifts."

20. Though he had not Fortunatus's Purse, the farmer had money and to spare, and when the harvest was gathered in, he bought a fine suit of clothes, and took his best horse and went to the royal city to see the sights.

21. The pomp and splendour, the festivities and fine clothes dazzled him.
22. "This is a gay life which these young courtiers lead," said he. "A man has nothing to do but to enjoy himself."

23. "If he has plenty of gold in his pocket," said a bystander.
24. By and by the Princess passed in her carriage. She was the King's only daughter. She had hair made of sunshine, and her eyes were stars.

25. "What an exquisite creature!" cried the farmer. "What would not one give to possess her?"
26. "She has as many suitors as hairs on her head," replied the bystander. "She wants to marry the Prince of Moonshine, but he only dresses in silver, and the King thinks he might find a richer son-in-law. The Princess will go to the highest bidder."

27. "And I have Good Luck for my godfather, and am not even at court!" cried the farmer; and he put spurs to his horse, and rode home.

Part 3

28. Good Luck was taking care of the farm.
29. "Listen, Godfather!" cried the young man. "I am in love with the King's daughter, and would want her to wife."

30. "It is not an easy matter," replied Good Luck, "but I will do what I can for you. Say that by good luck you saved the Princess's life, or perhaps better the King's—for they say he is selfish—"

31. "Tush!" cried the farmer. "The King is covetous, and wants a rich son-in-law."
32. "A wise man may bring wealth to a kingdom with his head, if not with his hands," said Good Luck, "and I can show you a district where the earth only wants mining to be flooded with wealth. Besides, there are a thousand opportunities that can be turned to account and influence. By wits and work, and with Good Luck to help him, many a poorer man than you has risen to greatness."

33. "Wits and work!" cried the indignant godson. "You speak well—truly! A hillman would have made a better godfather. Give me as much gold as will fill three meal-bins, and you may keep the rest of your help for those who want it."

34. Now at this moment by Good Luck stood Dame Fortune. She likes handsome young men, and there was some little jealousy between her and the godfather so she smiled at the quarrel.

35. "You would rather have had me for your gossip?" said she.
36. "If you would give me three wishes, I would," replied the farmer boldly, "and I would trouble you no more."
37. "Will you make him over to me?" said Dame Fortune to the godfather.
38. "If he wishes it," replied Good Luck. "But if he accepts your gifts, he has no further claim on me."
39. "Nor on me either," said the Dame. "Hark ye, young man, you mortals are apt to make a hobble of your three wishes, and you may end with a sausage at your nose, like your betters."

40. "I have thought of it too often," replied the farmer, "and I know what I want. For my first wish I desire imperishable beauty."

41. "It is yours," said Dame Fortune, smiling as she looked at him.
42. "The face of a prince and the manners of a clown are poor partners," said the farmer. "My second wish is for suitable learning and courtly manners, which cannot be gained at the plough-tail."

43. "You have them in perfection," said the Dame, as the young man thanked her by a graceful bow.
44. "Thirdly," said he, "I demand a store of gold that I can never exhaust."
45. "I will lead you to it," said Dame Fortune; and the young man was so eager to follow her that he did not even look back to bid farewell to his godfather.

Part 4

46. He was soon at court. He lived in the utmost pomp. He had a suit of armor made for himself out of beaten gold. No metal less precious might come near his person, except for the blade of his sword. This was obliged to be made of steel, for gold is not always strong enough to defend one's life or his honour. But the Princess still loved the Prince of Moonshine.

47. "Stuff and nonsense!" said the King. "I shall give you to the Prince of Gold."
48. "I wish I had the good luck to please her," muttered the young Prince. But he had not, for all his beauty and his wealth. However, she was to marry him, and that was something.

49. The preparations for the wedding were magnificent.
50. "It is a great expense," sighed the King, "but then I get the Prince of Gold for a son-in-law."

51. The Prince and his bride drove around the city in a triumphal procession. Her hair fell over her like sunshine, but the starlight of her eyes was cold.

52. In the train rode the Prince of Moonshine, dressed in silver, and with no color in his face.

53. As the bridal chariot approached one of the city gates, two black ravens hovered over it, and then flew away, and settled on a tree.

54. Good Luck was sitting under the tree to see his godson's triumph, and he heard the birds talking

above him.

55. "Has the Prince of Gold no friend who can tell him that there is a loose stone above the archway that is tottering to fall?" said they. And Good Luck covered his face with his mantle as the Prince drove through.

56. Just as they were passing out of the gateway the stone fell on to the Prince's head. He wore a casque of pure gold, but his neck was broken.

57. "We can't have all this expense for nothing," said the King: so he married his daughter to the Prince of Moonshine. If one can't get gold, one must be content with silver.

58. "Will you come to the funeral?" asked Dame Fortune of the godfather.
59. "Not I," replied Good Luck. "I had no hand in this matter."
60. The rain came down in torrents. The black feathers on the ravens' backs looked as if they had been oiled.
61. "Caw! caw!" said they. "It was an unlucky end."

13. What happens when the son goes into town? Circle the correct answer choice

    Ⓐ He goes to a party and celebrates his wealth.
    Ⓑ He saw the Princess and is intrigued to find out more about her.
    Ⓒ He meets a beggar.
    Ⓓ None of the above.

14. What did the farmer ask Dame Fortune to do? Write a sentence to explain your answer.

> **Question 15 is based on the poem below**

FOREIGN LANDS

Up into the cherry tree
Who should climb but little me?
I held the trunk with both my hands
And looked abroad on foreign lands.

I saw the next-door garden lie,
Adorned with flowers, before my eye,
And many pleasant faces more
That I had never seen before.

I saw the dimpling river pass
And be the sky's blue looking-glass;
The dusty roads go up and down
With people tramping into town.

If I could find a higher tree
Farther and farther I should see,
To where the grown-up river slips
Into the sea among the ships.

To where the roads on either hand
Lead onward into fairyland,
Where all the children dine at five,
And all the playthings come alive.

- By Robert Louis Stevenson

15. **Reading poetry can often help you to draw pictures in your mind. Reread the poem again and see if you can draw at least one picture in your mind.**
   Illustrate (draw) or write about what image or images come to mind when you read this poem."

CHAPTER 1 → Lesson 3: Caring Characters & Life Lessons

Question 1 is based on the paragraph below

A thirsty crow found a pitcher with just a little water in the bottom. His long, slender beak could just touch the water, but he could not get a drink. Looking around, the crow noticed many small stones lying nearby. Patiently, he picked up the stones one by one, and filled the pitcher until the water was high enough for him to get a drink.

1. What is the moral of this fable?

- Ⓐ Haste makes waste.
- Ⓑ Where there's a will, there's a way.
- Ⓒ Look before you leap.
- Ⓓ He who hesitates is lost.

Question 2 and 3 are based on the story below

After reading the story, enter the details in the map below. This will help you to answer the questions that follow.

Eight-year-old Tess heard her parents talking about her little brother Andrew. She realized something was wrong. Andrew was very sick, and they did not have enough money for his treatment. Tess heard her daddy say, "Only a miracle can save him now."

Tess went to her bedroom and retrieved a jar from its hiding place. There were a few coins in it. She counted them carefully. She then made her way to the drug store. The pharmacist was too busy to pay attention to her. "And what do you want?" he asked, annoyed at her persistence. "Can't you see that I am talking to my brother? He is here from Chicago."

Tess persisted, "My brother's really sick .... and I want to buy a miracle. His name is Andrew. He has something bad growing inside of his head and my daddy says only a miracle can save him now. So, how much does a miracle cost?" Tess rambled.

The pharmacist's brother, a well-dressed man, stooped down and asked the girl. "What kind of miracle does your brother need?"

"Don't know," replied Tess, eyes welling up with tears. "I just know Mommy says he needs an operation. But my daddy can't pay for it. So, I want to use my money."

The man from Chicago asked, "How much money do you have?"

"One dollar and eleven cents," said Tess.

"Well, what a coincidence," smiled the man.

"One dollar and eleven cents is the exact price of a miracle for your little brother." He took her money in one hand and grasped Tess's hand in the other. "Take me to where you live. I want to see your brother and meet your parents. Let's see if I have the kind of miracle you need."

The well-dressed man was Carlton Armstrong, a neurosurgeon. He operated on Andrew without charging any money. It wasn't long until Andrew was home and well again. "I wonder how much the surgery cost?" said Mother.

Tess smiled to herself. She knew exactly how much the miracle cost— one dollar and eleven cents.... plus the immense faith of a little child.

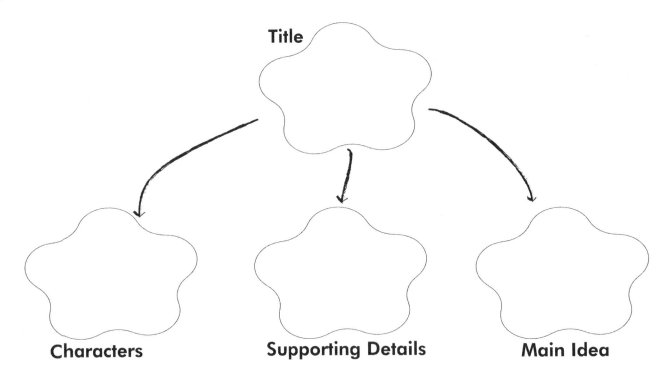

2. What is the message of this story?

Ⓐ Parents care for their kids.
Ⓑ Take good care of your health.
Ⓒ Worrying solves problems.
Ⓓ Miracles can happen when one has faith.

3. What is the moral of the above story?

Ⓐ Tess was an eight-year-old girl.
Ⓑ Sick people always get better by miracles.
Ⓒ Miracles always happen.
Ⓓ Persistence is more likely to get you what you want rather than doing nothing at all.

Question 4 is based on the fables below

A. Once a gazelle was running as fast as she could to outrun a lion who was pursuing her. She had a good lead and was probably going to outrun the lion when she came to a river. Although she could swim, the water looked cold and uninviting. She hesitated on the bank of the river, not wanting to jump in. While she debated, the lion overtook her, and she became his dinner.

B. Once a gazelle was running as fast as she could to outrun a lion who was pursuing her. She had a good lead and was probably going to outrun the lion when she came to a river. Without look-ing, she jumped into the water where a crocodile was waiting, and she became his dinner.

4. Part A

What is the moral of Fable A?

Ⓐ He who hesitates is lost.
Ⓑ Look before you leap.
Ⓒ Running away never solves the problem.
Ⓓ One's actions do not determine one's fate.

4. Part B

What is the moral of Fable B?

Ⓐ He who hesitates is lost.
Ⓑ Look before you leap.
Ⓒ One's actions do not reflect one's fate.
Ⓓ Running away never solves the problem.

5. Which moral best completes the following story?

A dog that was prone to biting, was given a loud bell to wear around its neck. When anyone heard the bell, they quickly turned and went in the other direction. The dog was very proud of his bell until the old owl told him, _____.

   Ⓐ Liars are not believed, even when they tell the truth.
   Ⓑ Birds of a feather flock together.
   Ⓒ Better half of a meal in freedom that a full meal in chains.
   Ⓓ To be well known is not always to be admired.

6. Which moral best completes the following story?

The boy who guarded the sheep for the village was often bored and lonely. Once or twice, he called out, "Wolf!" just so the villagers would come out into the field to help him. He laughed to see them so excited. But one day, a wolf came to where the sheep were grazing. The boy called loudly, "Wolf! Wolf!" but no one from the village came to help him. _____

   Ⓐ Liars are not believed, even when they tell the truth.
   Ⓑ Birds of a feather flock together.
   Ⓒ Better half of a meal in freedom that a full meal in chains.
   Ⓓ To be well known is not always to be admired.

Question 7 and 8 are based on the fables below

A.   The king's dinner was to be an elaborate affair, with many guests. In the kitchen, the cooks were rushing to prepare an elegant dinner. Extra chefs had been brought in from all over the kingdom and everyone was working very hard. The first dish on the menu was a delicate soup, full of fresh vegetables from the king's own garden. Each time a cook walked by and smelled the soup, he would taste it, and add just a pinch of salt to bring out the flavor. After each cook had added just a pinch of salt, the soup was served to the king, who sent it back to the kitchen. Too salty!

B.   The king's dinner was to be an elaborate affair, with many guests. In the kitchen, the cooks were rushing to prepare an elegant dinner. Extra chefs had been brought in from all over the kingdom and everyone was working very hard. The first dish on the menu was a delicate soup, full of fresh vegetables from the king's own garden. Many vegetables had to be chopped into tiny pieces, but because there were so many helpers in the kitchen, the soup was easy to prepare. When the king tasted the rich soup, he declared it to be a magnificent piece of work.

7. Which of the following is the moral of Fable A?

   Ⓐ Many hands make light work.
   Ⓑ Too many cooks spoil the broth.
   Ⓒ Never trust a cook who doesn't eat his own soup.
   Ⓓ A king can never be satisfied.

8. Which of the following is the moral of Fable B?

Ⓐ Many hands make light work.
Ⓑ Too many cooks spoil the broth.
Ⓒ Never trust a cook who doesn't eat his own soup.
Ⓓ A King can never be satisfied.

Question 9 is based on the poem below

A spring morning
A strong breeze
Squirrels gaze lazily
Bud covered trees.
Many new born critters
An orange streaked dawn
Birds chirping happily
Wet lawn.
Rain coats and tees
Smell of fresh bloomed flowers
Buzzing of pollen seeking bees
Kites soaring in the sky.
Games at the park
Tractor drives across the field
Refreshing lemonade
What will this year's crops yield?
Dewy mornings
Afternoon rain showers
Muggy nights
Nature's beauty overpowers...
......Spring Happenings

9. What statement best summarizes this poem?

Ⓐ Spring is an uncomfortable season for some people.
Ⓑ Spring is about new life and new beginnings.
Ⓒ Spring comes after winter.
Ⓓ Spring is followed by summer.

Question 10 is based on the story below

The Adventures of Huckleberry Finn by Mark Twain

Excerpt- public domain

I wanted to go and look at a place right about the middle of the island that I'd found when I was exploring; so we started and soon got to it, because the island was only three miles long and a quarter of a mile wide.

This place was a tolerable long, steep hill or ridge about forty feet high. We had a rough time getting to the top, the sides were so steep and the bushes so thick. We tramped and clumb around all over it, and by and by found a good big cavern in the rock, most up to the top on the side towards Illinois. The cavern was as big as two or three rooms bunched together, and Jim could stand up straight in it. It was cool in there. Jim was for putting our traps in there right away, but I said we didn't want to be climbing up and down there all the time.

Jim said if we had the canoe hid in a good place, and had all the traps in the cavern, we could rush there if anybody was to come to the island, and they would never find us without dogs. And, besides, he said them little birds had said it was going to rain, and did I want the things to get wet?

So, we went back, and got the canoe, and paddled up abreast the cavern, and lugged all the traps up there. Then we hunted up a place close by to hide the canoe in, amongst the thick willows. We took some fish off of the lines and set them again, and begun to get ready for dinner.

The door of the cavern was big enough to roll a hogshead in, and on one side of the door the floor stuck out a little bit, and was flat and a good place to build a fire on. So we built it there and cooked dinner.

10. What details in the story tell you that the island was not very big? Write down the details that you find.

Excerpt from Jo's Boys
Chapter 1 - Ten Years Later
by Louisa May Alcott

"If anyone had told me what wonderful changes were to take place here in ten years, I wouldn't have believed it." said Mrs. Jo to Mrs. Meg, as they sat on the piazza at Plumfield one summer day, looking about them with faces full of pride and pleasure.

"This is the sort of magic that money and kind hearts can work. I am sure Mr. Laurence could have no nobler monument than the college he so generously endowed; and a home like this will keep Aunt March's memory green as long as it lasts". Answered Mrs. Meg, always glad to praise the absent.
"We used to believe in fairies, you remember, and plan what we'd ask for if we could have three wishes. Doesn't it seem as if mine had been really granted at last? Money, fame, and plenty of the work I love," said Mrs. Jo, carelessly rumpling up her hair as she clasped her hands over her head just as she used to do when a girl.

"I have had mine, and Amy is enjoying hers to her heart's content. If dear Marmee, John, and Beth were here, it would be quite perfect,"added Meg, with a tender quiver in her voice; for Marmee's place was empty now.
Jo put her hand on her sister's, and both sat silent for a little while, surveying the pleasant scene before them with mingled sad and happy thoughts.

Something magical happened in a quiet place called Plumfield. Everything changed. The house became even more welcoming with fresh paint, new wings, and a beautiful garden. It looked prosperous and happy, unlike before when there were noisy boys running around and the Bhaers had a hard time making enough money. On top of the hill, where people used to fly kites, there was now a wonderful college. Students were busy walking along the paths that used to be for playing. They were getting lots of knowledge and enjoying the good things that come with wealth, wisdom, and kindness.

11. **Visualize the scene described in this selection. If you were to make a drawing or painting, what would you do to be sure to include to help someone understand your thoughts? List 3 things to include based on the details of the passage.**

A GOOD PLAY

We built a ship upon the stairs,
All made of the back-bedroom chairs,
And filled it full of sofa pillows
To go a-sailing on the billows.
We took a saw and several nails,
And water in the nursery pails;
And Tom said, "Let us also take
An apple and a slice of cake";
—
Which was enough for Tom and me
To go a-sailing on, till tea.
We sailed along for days and days,
And had the very best of plays;
But Tom fell out and hurt his knee,
So there was no one left but me.

-By Robert Louis Stevenson
www.gutenburg.com public domain

12. **After reading this poem, what can you conclude about what happened?**
    Circle the correct answer choice.

  Ⓐ Two boys were using their imagination while playing with make-believe ships on the stairs
     when one fell and was hurt.
  Ⓑ The poet likes to build ships everywhere.
  Ⓒ The boys played for days and days in the sea.
  Ⓓ Both B and C.

CHAPTER 1 → Lesson 4: Calling All Characters

Question 1 and 2 are based on the story below

After reading the story, enter the details in the map below. This will help you to answer the questions that follow.

Margaret was a simple lady who lived in a village with her husband, Robert. They had a daughter named Amy. Every day at sunrise, Margaret would wake up, cook, clean, and feed the cattle. Robert would milk the cows and then take the dogs for a long walk. Amy would study, help her mother for some time, and then get ready for school.

Amy studied in a school that was far away from her house, but she loved going to school. She went with her friends, Ingrid and Rebecca. They would walk together chatting, laughing, and singing songs as they went. They had to cross a river on the way. The only way they could cross it was by walking on a narrow bridge.

One day Margaret, Robert, Amy, and her friends were walking on the narrow bridge one behind the other. Amy and her friends were off to school, as usual, Margaret and Robert wanted to go to the market on the other side of the river to buy groceries for the house.

As they were crossing the narrow bridge, Rebecca slipped. She gave a frightened scream, clutching Ingrid, who was in front of her. Both of them lost their balance and fell into the river. Amy clutched her mother in fright. For a moment, she hesitated and then threw herself into the river after her friends, determined to save them.

Margaret screamed, and Robert jumped into the river. Some passers-by also jumped into the river and rescued the children, who were dripping wet, and shivering with fright.

That night, Robert patted his daughter Amy, and said, "You are a brave girl Amy, I'm proud of you."

Title

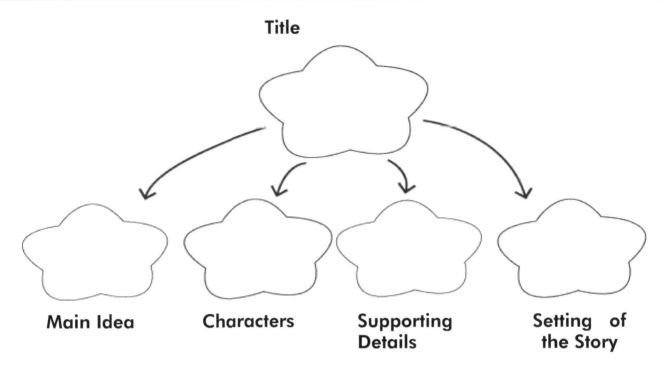

Main Idea   Characters   Supporting Details   Setting of the Story

1. In this story, Amy was scared but she jumped into the river. What caused Amy to ignore her fear?

Ⓐ Amy wanted to show off.
Ⓑ Amy wanted to escape.
Ⓒ Amy wanted to save her friends.
Ⓓ Amy wanted to join the fun.

2. Why did Robert jump into the river?

Ⓐ He wanted to save the girls.
Ⓑ He wanted to go for a swim.
Ⓒ He wanted to bathe in the river.
Ⓓ He was feeling hot.

After reading the story, enter the details in the map below. This will help you to answer the questions that follow.

One day, a baby elephant was happily dancing through the jungle, nodding his head and lifting his trunk to trumpet loudly.

The loud sound woke up a monkey who was sleeping in a tree nearby. He was very angry. He scolded the elephant and asked him to keep quiet.

"You silly animal," he said. "Can't you keep quiet? I'm sleeping."

"Oh, sorry," said the little elephant, and walked on. After some time, the little elephant reached a river and saw some beautiful swans there. He gazed at the beautiful birds. The swans looked at him and began to laugh.

"Oh! Look at that big creature," they said. "What a long nose, his ears are like fans, and look at his skin, it's much too big for him. He looks like a big wrinkled bag with all of those folds!" They laughed at him and swam away.

The little elephant was very sad. He tried to smooth out his skin with his trunk, but it was no good. He thought, "Why am I so ugly? Let me hide so that no one can see me."

He tried to hide in a thick bush, but he disturbed some nests. The birds flew above his head, crying loudly while trying to peck at him.

The little elephant ran for cover. He went behind a big rock to hide. Suddenly, he saw a big bear coming towards him. It was growling and appeared to be very angry. The little elephant was very frightened and trumpeted loudly. Just as he trumpeted, he heard a loud crashing and stomping. A herd of elephants came charging to the rescue you. You're so mighty and strong," he continued.

"But you are," replied the elephants. "You're a perfect little elephant." The little elephant danced for joy, he trumpeted loudly, and walked away happily with the other elephants following behind.

Title

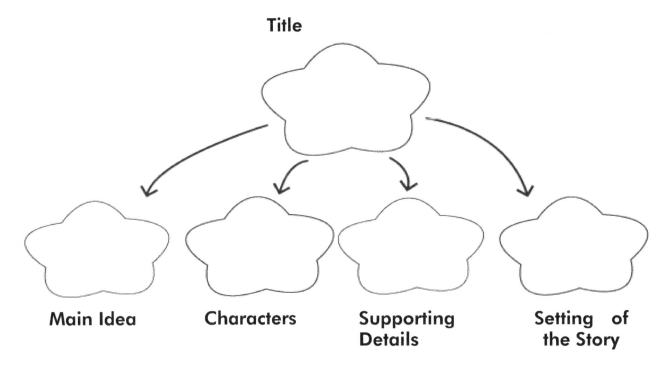

| Main Idea | Characters | Supporting Details | Setting of the Story |

3. Which of the little elephant's actions showed it was happy?

Ⓐ   It danced along happily.
Ⓑ   It was walking thoughtfully.
Ⓒ   It was swaying from side to side.
Ⓓ   It was sleeping peacefully.

4. Why does the little elephant tell the other elephants, "I wish I could be like you"?

Ⓐ   He loved the elephants.
Ⓑ   He admired them because they were mighty and strong.
Ⓒ   He was not an elephant.
Ⓓ   He was frightened of them.

After reading the story, enter the details in the map below. This will help you to answer the questions that follow.

Once upon a time, there was a wealthy woman that had very poor eyesight. She decided to call a doctor to ask if he could restore her eyesight. The doctor promised to cure her but told her that she had to pay him a huge fee. He also told her that throughout the treatment she had to keep her eyes closed. The woman agreed to both requirements.

The doctor began the treatment in the woman's home. Every day the doctor stole something from the lady's house. The treatment continued a lengthy period of time. Finally, when he had emptied her house, the doctor told her that he had finished her treatment and that her eyesight was restored. The woman was very happy that the treatment was over, but she refused to pay the doctor. The doctor was very angry that she refused to pay his hefty fee. He told her that he was taking her to court. She just laughed at him.

When the judge asked the woman to explain why she didn't pay the doctor, the woman said, "Sir, before the operation, I was partially blind, but at least I could see the things in my home." She continued, "But now after the treatment, I am unable to see anything in my home. The woman solemnly told the judge, I must be totally blind because I can see nothing."

The judge looked at the doctor, who hung his head in shame. The doctor realized that the woman knew that he had stolen all her things. He felt ashamed and returned everything he had stolen. The doctor also said the woman did not owe him a fee for the treatment.

5. Why did the doctor tell the old woman, "You must keep your eyes closed during the treatment"?

   Ⓐ   He wanted her to relax.
   Ⓑ   He did not want her to see him stealing the things from her house.
   Ⓒ   He could perform the operation better.
   Ⓓ   She would get her eyesight faster if she closed her eyes.

Question 6 is based on the story below

After reading the story, enter the details in the map below. This will help you to answer the questions that follow.

Brandon lived with his mother at one end of the forest. His school was at the other end of the forest. Every day he had to go through the forest to get to school and the forest was very scary.

One day he told his mother that he felt very scared to cross that forest. His mother said, "Don't be scared" "Your brother lives in the forest. Whenever you get scared, you can always call him. He won't answer you but he will see that no harm comes to you."

"Why did you not tell me about my brother earlier? What is his name?"

Mother said, "His name is Courage. Whenever you get frightened, call his name, and he will silently follow you to school and see that you come back home safely."

The next day Brandon was happy to get ready for school. He was not scared as he went through the forest on the way to school. That day, while coming home from school, he got scared when he heard the sounds of animals. He then remembered his mother's words that his brother would protect him whenever he was frightened. Brandon called out "Courage, Courage" with full confidence. Suddenly he began to feel better. He began to feel brave. He again called out, "Courage!, Courage!" He thought that his brother was silently following him, he began to sing softly and then loudly. He realized that he was not frightened after all. He crossed the forest confidently with courage.

The only thing we need to have is confidence and courage in ourselves to move ahead.

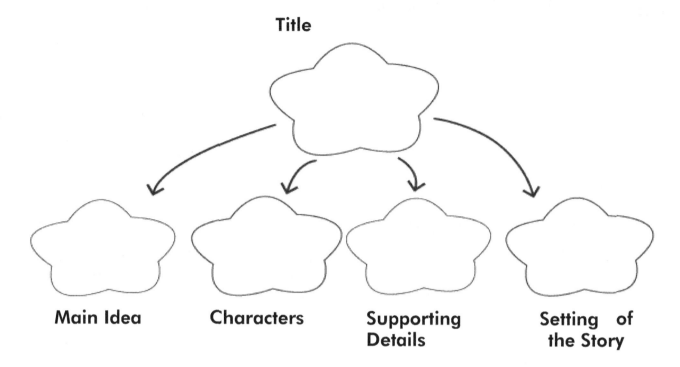

Title

Main Idea   **Characters**   **Supporting Details**   **Setting of the Story**

6. Why did Brandon begin to feel brave?

Ⓐ   He fought with the animals and won.
Ⓑ   He began to walk around the forest instead of through the forest.
Ⓒ   He found courage and confidence.
Ⓓ   He stopped going to school.

Question 7 is based on the paragraph below

How can I describe the creature that I have taken such pains to form? He was horrifying in every way. So wild were my thoughts that I seemed to see him everywhere. When at last I encountered him again, he said, "Remember, you have made me bigger and more powerful than you. Do not try to harm me. Be kind to me, as you should. Remember that I am your creature. I ought to be your son, but you rejected me for no reason. I was once good and kind, but everywhere I went people hated and feared me because of my hideous appearance. Misery has made me evil."

7. Which of the following does NOT describe the monster?

Ⓐ   He was frightening.
Ⓑ   He was strong.
Ⓒ   He was gentle.
Ⓓ   He was large.

After reading the story, enter the details in the map below. This will help you to answer the questions that follow.

My First Trip to the Beach

About three weeks ago, Jeremiah's parents surprised him with some news. They were taking him to the beach. He was excited and couldn't wait to tell all of his friends at school.

Soon enough, Friday afternoon arrived. Jeremiah, his sister, his parents, and his nanny all loaded into the car, and set out for the long drive to Destin, Florida. Listening to DVD's grew old rather quickly. A nap was sure to allow Jeremiah to get closer to Florida without growing bored from the ride.

When he awoke from his nap, it was time to stop for dinner. He exited the car, excited to stretch his legs. "Come on, Jeremiah," exclaimed his nanny. He was glad that she had been able to come to the beach. This was also going to be her first time seeing the ocean.

After a quick meal at a fast-food restaurant, the family piled back into the car.

The family arrived at their condo, almost too tired to enjoy the peaceful sound of the ocean. As Jeremiah headed to bed, he knew that the beach would be his to explore in a few hours. He stretched out his small frame across the twin-sized bed and soon fell asleep. He awoke a few hours later, hearing his dad outside on the balcony.

When Jeremiah finally saw the view in the daylight, he was in awe. Beautiful green waters lay off in the distance. They seemed to go on and on, as far as his eyes could see. The sand reminded him of snow.

"Wanna go for a walk?" asked his dad.

Jeremiah smiled, "Yes!" Running back inside, he threw his shoes on. His dad said that he didn't want to try to wear those in the soft, grainy sand. He dressed, and then off they went.

"What's this?" asked Jeremiah, pointing to a loose mound of sand.

"This is a sand dune, it keeps the buildings safe," his dad replied.

"Oh, okay..." Jeremiah and his dad walked along the ocean's edge. There were few words spoken, but the looks on their faces expressed feelings of happiness, as they walked along the beautiful water's edge.

Title

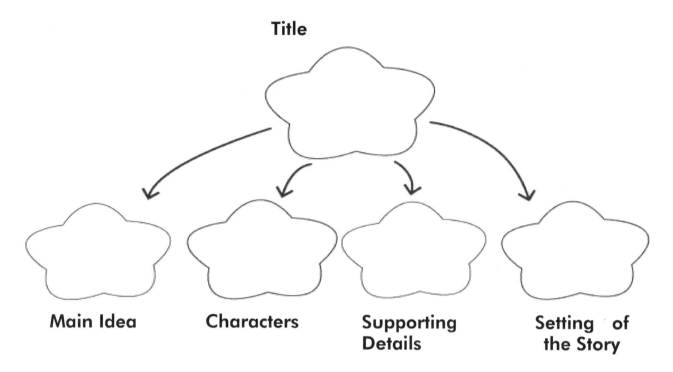

Main Idea   Characters   Supporting Details   Setting of the Story

8. Which statement BEST describes Jeremiah?

  Ⓐ He had traveled a lot.
  Ⓑ He was not familiar with the beach.
  Ⓒ He was very moody.
  Ⓓ He always had to have his way.

Question 9 and 10 are based on the story below

After reading the story, enter the details in the map below. This will help you to answer the questions that follow.

Danny had always been a different kind of child, so I wasn't real happy when Xavier started hanging out with him. I didn't really know how to handle the situation, but I didn't want to be one of those parents who told him he had to stop. When Xavier told me about playing with Danny that first day at recess, I remember thinking, "Oh no…"

It has been about a month since that day, and every afternoon I still ask if anyone lost recess today. It is my way of finding out if Danny or Xavier got into any trouble. This way it doesn't seem like I am pointing the finger at Danny. Those first few times that I asked, it seemed that Xavier would usually tell me something silly that Danny did to get in trouble: throws pit balls, spit wads, pour milk onto another student's mashed potatoes, run in the hallway, etc. Not bad things, just things that showed disrespect. As the days passed, either Xavier realized that I was fed up with Danny's silliness or wasn't Danny getting into as much trouble.

I have agreed to let Danny spend the night tonight. The boys are excited about sleeping outside in the tent, and I have arranged for them to make S'mores, have a small campfire, and enjoy the comforts of almost being alone in the wilderness. "Mom, where are you? This is Danny." I stare at Danny. He looks sweet enough. His short haircut makes him look much younger than eight, well, assuming that he is the same age as Xavier.

"Hi, Mrs."
"Just call me Ann. Danny, do you want to see Xavier's room?" I asked.

Danny smiled at me and I was hooked. His crystal blue eyes lit up, and his left cheek had a small, but noticeable dimple. I patted Danny on the back. "We are glad you came to visit," I stated. I walked the boys down the hallway to Xavier's room.

"What's this?" Xavier asked.
"Since this is your first official camp out, I thought you needed the right pajamas. I just guessed your size, Danny; let's hope they fit." Danny scooped the pajamas up, while Xavier shrugged.

"Is this the bathroom?" I nodded. Moments later, Danny returned, wearing his new pajamas. They were a little large, but they would do. The boy that I had pegged to be the troublemaker seemed so sweet. He threw his tiny arms around me. "These are great…" said Danny. I could see the tears in his eyes, and I pulled him even closer.

"I am glad you like them, Danny," I stated.

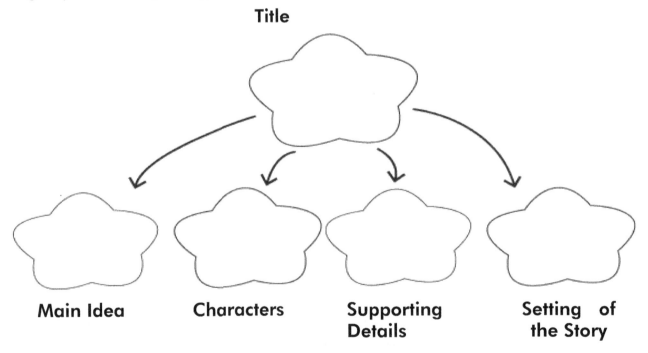

Title

Main Idea   **Characters**   **Supporting Details**   **Setting of the Story**

9. Which word BEST describes Xavier's mom?

Ⓐ harsh
Ⓑ unforgiving
Ⓒ open-minded
Ⓓ sad

10. How were Danny and Xavier different?

Ⓐ Danny often gets in trouble, while Xavier follows the rules.
Ⓑ Danny follows the rules, while Xavier often gets in trouble.
Ⓒ Xavier lives with his mom, but Danny does not.
Ⓓ Both boys are very much alike, which is why their mom wanted them to be friends.

Question 11 and 12 are based on the story below

Maggie's Dilemma?

Maggie has many things to accomplish over the weekend. She wants to go to a friend's house for a party on Sunday afternoon. If she doesn't get her chores and homework done, she is afraid that her parents will not let her attend the party.

As she is getting ready for bed, Friday night, she is worrying and wondering how she can do everything before the party on Sunday. Her mother tells her that she needs to prioritize her life. Maggie is not sure what that means. She thinks to herself, "What is prioritize? How does that help me in my life?"

Her older brother, Ronny, comes into her room. He asks her, "Hey, Sis, why the puzzled look? Why are you just sitting there on your bed looking around your room?"

"Ronny, what does it mean when Mom tells me I need to prioritize my life?"
"What's wrong with my life?"

Ron laughs and tells her that she has a tendency to try to do too much stuff in too little time. He suggests that she make a list of what she needs to do. Then, she needs to make a list of what she wants to do. Again, Maggie looks confused.

He takes out one of her notebooks and starts to write. She watches as he puts his name at the top of the list along with the words - Have to Do. Then he makes numbers going down each side. He writes, clean room as number 1. For number 2, he puts down take out the trash. Ron then writes down, mow the yard for number 3.

On another sheet of paper, he does the same thing, only this time after his name, he writes- Want to Do. On the second list, the number 1 is watch wrestling on TV. Number 2 is play video games.

Suddenly, Maggie gets it! "Oh, I see now. Prioritize means to put things in order of importance."

Her brother replies, "Duh, I knew I could help out!" Ron laughs along with Maggie. She is no longer puzzled and starts to write.

11. What was the problem that Maggie was having? Select the correct answer by circling it.

Ⓐ She kept her room too messy.
Ⓑ She couldn't decide what her brother wanted her to do.
Ⓒ Maggie did not know how she could do everything she needed to do and wanted to do over the weekend.
Ⓓ None of the above.

12. What do you think Maggie will do next?
Write at least 3 sentences to tell what you think she will do next based on this story. Be sure to use complete sentences in your answer.

Bringing a Bear to School

Tyrone was so happy that his teacher said they were going to have a special celebration for a unit they had been studying on Bears in his class. They had been reading many bear books lately. Some of the books were about real bears and some were books about make-believe bears like Paddington and others. Mr. Clark, his teacher, wanted the students to relate to their own real-life experiences. The students were talking about the celebration during class one day.

Mr. Clark told them they could bring a stuffed bear from home if they wanted to or another stuffed animal for the day of the celebration. The girls were all excited. The boys were laughing and snickering about how dumb that idea was. They were saying only sissies would bring or have a stuffed toy. Tyrone's mouth frowned. He loved his Beary. He had Beary since he was just a tiny baby. Tyrone's grandfather had brought it to his mom on the day Tyrone was born. His grandfather had passed away several years later, and Tyrone held Beary all the time he thought about his grandfather. He even saved his allowance and special birthday money to buy his stuffed bear clothes. When Tyrone joined the soccer team, Beary got a soccer outfit. When he joined t-ball, Beary got a baseball uniform, too. So why were the boys making fun of having a stuffed bear? Tyrone did not understand.

The teacher sent home a note the weekend before the celebration explaining to parents what the next school day (Monday) would be like. Mr. Clark said that the students could bring their own stuffed animal if they chose to do so for a show and tell part of the celebration. They were even having zoo personnel come and share their experiences with the bears at the zoo. There would be Bear shaped cookies and cakes, too! Mr. Clark was also bringing his video of his trip to Russia where he saw many polar bears.

It sounded like so much fun! But, Tyrone was still hesitant on whether or not he should bring Beary to school. He wanted to show him off with his clothes and all. He wanted to tell the story of how his grandfather bought him the bear and how much it means to him still.

When Tyrone got home from school on Friday afternoon, he showed his mom the note from Mr. Clark. He had a puzzled look on his face. His mom said it sounded like the class was going to have a wonderful time on Monday. His sister, LaTasha, started laughing loudly. "Oh, please tell me you are not thinking of taking Beary?" she exclaimed.

"I was, but the other boys would probably make fun of me."
His mom said, "Why would they do that, Tyrone? Don't you think they have stuffed animals, too?"
"Maybe mom, but they would never admit it or bring them to school."

So all weekend long, Tyrone pondered what to do. Right before bedtime on Sunday night, he made his decision. Beary and his outfits were ready to go!

On Monday morning, Tyrone's mom decided she would take him to school herself rather than have him walk or ride the bus. When they arrived at his class, Mr. Clark was greeting all of the classmates. The entire classroom was decorated with bears of all sorts. On the front of Mr. Clark's desk was a beautiful stuffed bear. A sign in front said, "My Buddy!" Tyrone grinned from ear to ear as he joyfully took out Beary, dressed him in his baseball uniform, and put him on his desk. He made his own sign, "My Beary!"

Needless to say it was a great day for Tyrone. Several of the other boys had brought their stuffed animals and stuffed bears, too.

13. **In your own words, write a sentence explaining what Beary means to Tyrone and why. Use the evidence in the story for your answer.**

CHAPTER 1 → Lesson 5: A Chain of Events

Question 1 is based on the story below

One day, a baby elephant was happily dancing through the jungle, nodding his head and lifting his trunk to trumpet loudly.

The loud sound woke up a monkey who was sleeping in a tree nearby. He was very angry. He scolded the elephant and asked him to keep quiet.

"You silly animal," he said. "Can't you keep quiet? I'm sleeping."

"Oh, sorry," said the little elephant, and walked on. After some time, the little elephant reached a river and saw some beautiful swans there. He gazed at the beautiful birds. The swans looked at him and began to laugh.

"Oh! Look at that big creature," they said. "What a long nose, his ears are like fans, and look at his skin, it's much too big for him. He looks like a big wrinkled bag with all of those folds!" They laughed at him and swam away.

The little elephant was very sad. He tried to smooth out his skin with his trunk, but it was no good. He thought, "Why am I so ugly? Let me hide so that no one can see me."

He tried to hide in a thick bush, but he disturbed some nests. The birds flew above his head, crying loudly while trying to peck at him.

The little elephant ran for cover. He went behind a big rock to hide. Suddenly, he saw a big bear coming towards him. It was growling and appeared to be very angry. The little elephant was very frightened and trumpeted loudly. Just as he trumpeted, he heard a loud crashing and stomping. A herd of elephants came charging to the rescue.

Seeing the herd, the frightened bear ran away.

The little elephant joyfully ran to the big elephants, thanked them, and said, "I wish I could be like you. You're so mighty and strong," he continued.

"But you are," replied the elephants. "You're a perfect little elephant." The little elephant danced for joy; he trumpeted loudly and walked away happily with the other elephants following behind.

1. Choose the correct set of words to fill in the blank.

Ⓐ He asks the bear to leave him.
Ⓑ He began to trumpet loudly.
Ⓒ He ran as fast as he could.
Ⓓ He was crying.

Question 2 is based on the story below

Margaret was a simple lady who lived in a village with her husband, Robert. They had a daughter named Amy. Every day at sunrise, Margaret would wake up, cook, clean, and feed the cattle. Robert would milk the cows and then take the dogs for a long walk. Amy would study, help her mother for some time, and then get ready for school.

Amy studied in a school that was far away from her house, but she loved going to school. She went with her friends, Ingrid and Rebecca. They would walk together chatting, laughing, and singing songs as they went. They had to cross a river on the way. The only way they could cross it was by walking on a narrow bridge.

One day Margaret, Robert, Amy, and her friends were walking on the narrow bridge one behind the other. Amy and her friends were off to school, as usual, Margaret and Robert wanted to go to the market on the other side of the river to buy groceries for the house.

As they were crossing the narrow bridge, Rebecca slipped. She gave a frightened scream, clutching Ingrid, who was in front of her. Both of them lost their balance and fell into the river. Amy clutched her mother in fright. For a moment she hesitated and then threw herself into the river after her friends, determined to save them.

Margaret screamed, and Robert jumped into the river. Some passers-by also jumped into the river and rescued the children, who were dripping wet and shivering with fright.

That night Robert patted his daughter Amy and said, "You are a brave girl Amy, I'm proud of you."

LumosLearning.com

2. What happened after Rebecca grabbed Ingrid on the bridge?

Ⓐ Margaret and Robert went on the other side of the river.
Ⓑ Robert screamed.
Ⓒ The girls fell into the river.
Ⓓ Margaret helped her family by cooking and cleaning.

3. Which of the following answers best shows the chain of events?

(1) I was very mad at my sister for eating the cookie.
(2) "Why did you eat the last cookie?" I asked.
(3) Sister ate the last cookie in the cookie jar.
(4) "Sorry," she said, "I was really hungry."

Ⓐ 3,1,4,2
Ⓑ 3,1,2,4
Ⓒ 1,2,3,4
Ⓓ 2,3,4,1

Question 4 is based on the poem below

I quarreled with my brother
I don't know what about,
One thing led to another
And somehow we fell out.
The start of it was slight,
The end of it was strong,
He said he was right,
I knew he was wrong!
We hated one another.
The afternoon turned black.
Then suddenly my brother
Thumped me on the back.
And said, "Oh, come along!
We can't go on all night-
I was in the wrong."
So he was in the right.

-by Eleanor Farjeon

4. Which event happened last in the poem?

Ⓐ The two brothers argued.
Ⓑ One brother apologized to the other.
Ⓒ The weather turned rainy.
Ⓓ The two brothers played together.

Question 5 is based on the passage below

Cell Phones in the Classroom

A familiar ringtone sounds in the classroom directing everyone's attention to a shy student in the back row. Several years ago, this would have seemed a bit strange, but not today. A recent study showed that one in three third-grade students have a cell phone. With so many students having access to technology devices, a lot of talks have gone into deciding whether to use them as learning tools or to ban them from the classroom.

Let's think about cell phones' role as learning tools. Annie needs a calculator but forgot hers. She takes out her cell phone and can use the calculator app on the phone. Just across the room, Johnny is trying to spell the word "similar," so he uses the dictionary app on his phone to find the correct spelling. Mitchell, has completed all of his work early, so he decides to use the multiplication app on his phone to review multiplication facts in a fun and interactive way. These devices are causing teachers and other school officials to see that cell phones give students access to resources that actually save schools money.

While cell phones may sound great, not every school district is ready to lift the cell phone ban. There are still those that have major concerns. One concern is what to do about students who do not have a cell phone. Another worry is how to make sure students are using the phone as a learning tool instead of texting and social media. Additional concerns arise with how to address when a phone is broken or stolen while at school. Certainly, the list of problems that some schools have goes on and on.

The answer isn't clear for schools across the United States. Some schools are starting to lift the cell phone ban, but others are keeping it in place. As students pack backpacks with cell phones, the discussion of having them in the classroom will certainly continue.

5. **According to the passage, what happened before Mitchell opened the multiplication app on his phone?**

   (A) His teacher told him to play outside.
   (B) He completed all of his assignments.
   (C) He got bored.
   (D) He heard an alarm.

After reading the story, enter the details in the map below. This will help you to answer the questions that follow.

Danny had always been a different kind of child, so I wasn't real happy when Xavier started hanging out with him. I didn't really know how to handle the situation, but I didn't want to be one of those parents that told him he had to stop. When Xavier told me about playing with Danny that first day at recess, I remember thinking, "Oh no..."

It has been about a month since that day, and I still ask every afternoon if anyone lost recess today. It is my way of finding out if Danny or Xavier got into any trouble. This way it doesn't seem so much like I am pointing the finger at Danny. Those first few times that I asked, it seemed that Xavier was always telling me something silly that Danny did to get in trouble: spit wads, pouring his milk into another student's mashed potatoes, running in the hallway, etc. Not bad things, just things that showed disrespect. As the days passed, either Xavier has realized that I am fed up with Danny's silliness or he isn't getting in trouble as much.

I have agreed to let Danny spend the night tonight. The boys are excited about sleeping outside in the tent, and I have arranged for them to make S'mores, have a small campfire, and enjoy the comforts of almost being alone

in the wilderness. "Mom, where are you? This is Danny." I stare at Danny. He looks sweet enough. His short haircut makes him look much younger than his age of eight, well, assuming that he is the same age as Xavier.

"Hi, Mrs."
"Just call me Ann. Danny, do you want to see Xavier's room?" I asked.

Danny smiled at me and I was hooked. His crystal blue eyes lit up, and his left cheek had a small, but noticeable dimple. I patted Danny on the back. "We are glad you came to visit," I stated. I walked the boys down the hallway to Xavier's room.

"What's this?" Xavier asked.
"Since this is your first official camp out, I thought you needed the right pajamas. I just guessed your size, Danny; let's hope they fit." Danny scooped the pajamas up, while Xavier just shrugged.

"Is this the bathroom?" I nodded. Moments later, Danny returned, wearing his new pajamas. They were a little large, but they would do. The boy that I had pegged to be the troublemaker seemed so sweet. He threw his tiny arms around me. "These are great..." said Danny. I could see the tears in his eyes, and I pulled him even closer.

"I am glad you like them, Danny," I stated.

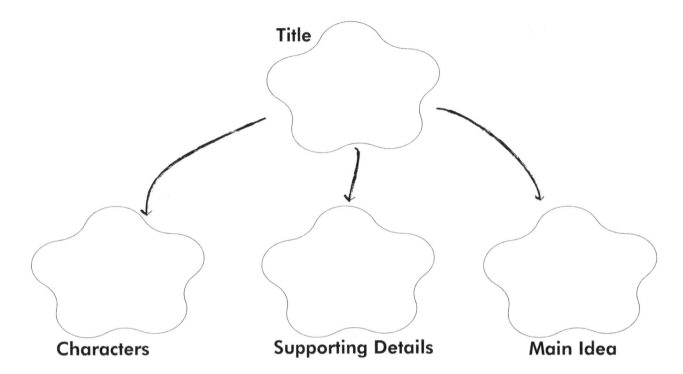

6. What can you infer was the reason Danny started to get in less trouble at school?

Ⓐ He got a new home.
Ⓑ He became friends with Xavier.
Ⓒ Danny's mom bought him some new pajamas.
Ⓓ He got sent to the principal's office.

7. What had Xavier's mom done before Danny arrived?

Ⓐ Put the tent up in Xavier's room.
Ⓑ Bought Danny some new pajamas.
Ⓒ Bought the items needed to make dinner.
Ⓓ Hid all her valuable items.

Question 8 is based on the story below

Once upon a time, there was a wealthy woman that had very poor eyesight. She decided to call a doctor to ask if he could restore her eyesight. The doctor promised to cure her but told her that she had to pay him a huge fee. He also told her that throughout the treatment she had to keep her eyes closed. The woman agreed to both requirements.

The doctor began the treatment in the woman's home. Every day the doctor stole something from the lady's house. The treatment lasted a lengthy period of time. Finally, when he had emptied her house, the doctor told her that he had finished her treatment and that her eyesight was restored.

The woman was very happy that the treatment was over, but she refused to pay the doctor. The doctor was very angry that she refused to pay his hefty fee. He told her that he was taking her to court. She just laughed at him.

When the judge asked the woman to explain why she didn't pay the doctor, the woman said, "Sir, before the operation, I was partially blind, but at least I could see the things in my home." She continued, "But now after the treatment, I am unable to see anything in my home. The woman solemnly told the judge, I must be totally blind because I can see nothing."

The judge looked at the doctor, who hung his head in shame. The doctor realized that the woman knew that he had stolen all her things. He felt ashamed and returned everything he had stolen. The doctor also said the woman did not owe him a fee for the treatment.

8. Choose the correct sentence that concludes the chain of events.

Ⓐ The judge made the old woman pay the doctor his fee.
Ⓑ The doctor paid the woman his fee.
Ⓒ The doctor refused to take his fees.
Ⓓ The doctor returned everything he had stolen.

Question 9 is based on the paragraph below

An astronomer used to go out every night to observe stars. Often, he would be seen with a telescope in one hand and a notebook in the other. One evening, while he wandered through the suburbs with his attention fixed on the sky, he accidentally fell into a deep uncovered well. He cried out loudly for help. As he waited to be rescued, he moaned and howled about his sores and bruises. His neighbor was passing by and happened to hear his wailing and weeping. He quickly helped him out of the well. After he came to know how the accident happened, this is what he said to the astronomer: "Hark you old fellow, why in striving to pry into heaven, do you not manage to see what is on earth?"

9. Which event happened first in the story?

Ⓐ A neighbor heard the astronomer fall in a well.
Ⓑ The neighbor helped the astronomer out of the well.
Ⓒ The neighbor yelled at the astronomer for not paying attention.
Ⓓ The astronomer went for a walk.

Question 10 is based on the story below

After reading the story, enter the details in the map below. This will help you to answer the questions that follow.

I Don't Want To Go

Emily zipped up her suitcase, sighed loudly, and then lugged it out to the Family Utility Vehicle. "Why do I have to go?" she asked.
"This is a family vacation," replied her dad.

Sure it was, she thought. The idea of spending three entire days and nights sleeping in a tent out in the wilderness that was named after the explorer Daniel Boone did not appeal to her girly side. "Mom, can we stay...?"

Before she could finish, Emily's younger brother came bolting out the door, his suitcase overflowing, and his momentum almost knocking her to the ground. "Let's go, let's go."

Emily climbed into the backseat, her MP3 player blasting loudly; at least she had some piece of civilization left. As they drove for what seemed like forever, Emily enjoyed peering out the window. As they got farther and farther away from the city, she began to catch glimpses of rabbits, squirrels, and various birds that she wasn't used to seeing. The tall buildings and annoying noises of the city began to be replaced by a peaceful quiet. She turned her music off, but kept the ear buds in place, as she didn't want anyone to know that she was enjoying the ride. Finally, she saw the sign: Welcome to the Daniel Boone National Forest.

"Can we hike to the falls?" her brother asked.
She exited the vehicle, declared that she was ready for a walk. She had heard about Cumberland Falls but had never actually seen them. Some of her classmates had mentioned that they were smaller, but

a lot like Niagara Falls. She had no desire to let the others know she was excited, but she hoped that her dad would say that they could go exploring.

Looking around her, she saw huge mountains that seemed to tower above the river below. This was much different from the small subdivision that she called home. Just maybe the next three days wouldn't be so bad. As she removed her earbuds, she smiled, as a small deer crossed the pathway several hundred feet in the distance. The first live deer that she had ever seen was when she was twelve. " Wow, this is really amazing! Let's take that walk, Dad."
"Really?" he asked.

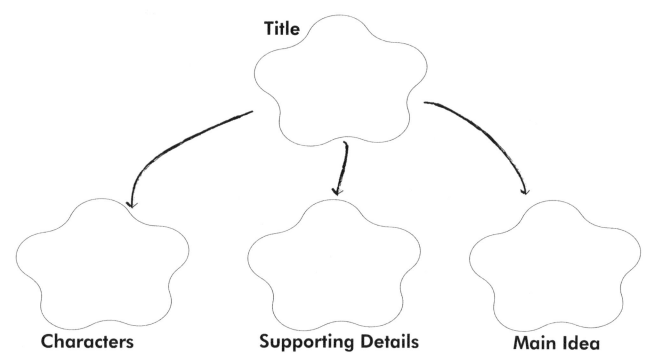

Title

Characters   **Supporting Details**   **Main Idea**

10. What happened to get Emily more interested in her camping trip with the family?

Ⓐ She listened to her MP3 player.
Ⓑ She saw a lot of wild animals that she was not used to seeing.
Ⓒ Her dad told her about a trip when he used to go camping with his parents.
Ⓓ Her brother started crying because he did not want her to be sad.

Christopher's Magic Reading Tricks!

There are many ways to help you in understanding things you read.
Here are some examples of ways that Christopher uses to help him in his reading.

The first one is what his teacher calls prior knowledge. This means that as you read you think -what do I already know if anything about this topic? Christopher says it helps him remember if he has ever read anything about it before. Then he uses that and tries to learn something new as he reads.

The second way is to question as you read. Think to yourself- what is the author trying to tell me, before, during and after you read? Christopher likes to say- "Self, what is it I am trying to learn as I read this? Can I repeat it after I read it?"

The third and Christopher says the most fun is to make a picture in your mind while you read. He says that if it is a story, you can even make a movie in your mind! Teachers use the term visualize your reading.

The fourth strategy or technique that Christopher learned from his teacher is to infer. This one means that Christopher has to use clues in the reading to figure out what is going on or what the author really means in the story.

The most favorite way for Christopher to get more out of what he has read is to summarize the reading. He tells his friends who may be struggling with this to tell what's important in a sentence or two after you read.

Christopher likes to reread his passages or stories more than one time when he knows he is going to be tested over them or asked questions about them. He says he also takes notes and sometimes uses more than one way to help him read better.

He had a hard time with reading when he was in first and second grade, but now since he uses these "magic tricks" to reading, he loves reading!

11. What is Christopher's favorite reading trick? Write your answer in the box given below.

Question 12 is based on the story below

Bringing a Bear to School

Tyrone was so happy that his teacher said they were going to have a special celebration for a unit they had been studying on Bears in his class. They had been reading many bear books lately. Some of the books were about real bears and some were books about make-believe bears like Paddington and others. Mr. Clark, his teacher, wanted the students to relate to their own real-life experiences. The students were talking about the celebration during class one day.

Mr. Clark told them they could bring a stuffed bear from home if they wanted to or another stuffed animal for the day of the celebration. The girls were all excited. The boys were laughing and snickering about how dumb that idea was. They were saying only sissies would bring or have a stuffed toy. Tyrone's mouth frowned. He loved his Beary. He had Beary since he was just a tiny baby. Tyrone's grandfather had brought it to his mom on the day Tyrone was born. His grandfather had passed away several years later, and Tyrone held Beary all the time he thought about his grandfather. He even saved his allowance and special birthday money to buy his stuffed bear clothes. When Tyrone joined the soccer team, Beary got a soccer outfit. When he joined t-ball, Beary got a baseball uniform, too. So why were the boys making fun of having a stuffed bear? Tyrone did not understand.

The teacher sent home a note the weekend before the celebration explaining to parents what the next school day (Monday) would be like. Mr. Clark said that the students could bring their own stuffed animal if they chose to do so for a show and tell part of the celebration. They were even having zoo personnel come and share their experiences with the bears at the zoo. There would be Bear shaped cookies and cakes, too! Mr. Clark was also bringing his video of his trip to Russia where he saw many polar bears.

It sounded like so much fun! But, Tyrone was still hesitant on whether or not he should bring Beary to school. He wanted to show him off with his clothes and all. He wanted to tell the story of how his grandfather bought him the bear and how much it means to him still.

When Tyrone got home from school on Friday afternoon, he showed his mom the note from Mr. Clark. He had a puzzled look on his face. His mom said it sounded like the class was going to have a wonderful time on Monday. His sister, LaTasha, started laughing loudly. "Oh, please tell me you are not thinking of taking Beary?" she exclaimed.

"I was, but the other boys would probably make fun of me."
His mom said, "Why would they do that, Tyrone? Don't you think they have stuffed animals, too?"
"Maybe mom, but they would never admit it or bring them to school."

So all weekend long, Tyrone pondered what to do. Right before bedtime on Sunday night, he made his decision. Beary and his outfits were ready to go!

On Monday morning, Tyrone's mom decided she would take him to school herself rather than have him walk or ride the bus. When they arrived at his class, Mr. Clark was greeting all of the classmates. The entire classroom was decorated with bears of all sorts. On the front of Mr. Clark's desk was a beautiful stuffed bear. A sign in front said, "My Buddy!" Tyrone grinned from ear to ear as he joyfully took out Beary, dressed him in his baseball uniform, and put him on his desk. He made his own sign, "My Beary!"

Needless to say it was a great day for Tyrone. Several of the other boys had brought their stuffed animals and stuffed bears, too.

12. Why did Mr. Clark decide to have a celebration for his class? Circle the correct answer choice.

Ⓐ It was his birthday and he wanted the students to have fun.
Ⓑ He liked celebrations.
Ⓒ The class was finishing a unit on bears and he wanted to wrap it up with real life experiences for the children.
Ⓓ None of the above.

Question 13 is based on the story below

Blue Hole

Sarah loved to go swimming at the local "Blue Hole" near her grandmother's house. The Blue Hole was nicknamed that because it was so crystal blue year round. It was located at the deep end of a creek bed. Regardless of whether it was winter, spring, summer or fall, the Blue Hole was ice cold, as well.

One early Saturday spring morning, Sarah, her friend Blaire, and her younger cousin Cody, were headed to the Blue Hole on their bikes. The traffic suddenly picked up and the old country gravel road was full of cars and trucks, even a few motorcycles. The kids all pulled off the road and stopped. "What is going on?" asked Sarah. Blaire replied, "I have no clue, no one is hardly ever on this road!" Just then Cody blurted out, "Look up ahead! Everyone is stopping at the Blue Hole. We will never get to swim now!"

Sure enough over 20 to 30 vehicles were stopped ahead and people were scrambling to the creek. "What do you think is happening?" questioned Sarah.

The kids dropped their bikes by the side of the road and ran ahead.

There it was! A baby calf had fallen into the icy Blue Hole and firefighters were struggling to get her out. News reporters were all around, as well. According to the reporter, the calf had been in the creek earlier that morning since before daybreak, but not at the Blue Hole end. The calf had gradually followed other people toward the deep end. Once there, she panicked and was unable to gain footing to get out.

The firefighters had been working to try to lasso her for over 2 hours, and were not having any luck. About that time, everyone heard a loud MOOOO! Over and over again and getting closer! It was the mother cow. She was looking for her baby! Instantly, the calf leaped to the edge of the creek bank. The mother cow came through the bushes rushing toward her baby. She licked and licked on her and the baby leaned against its mother. All was well, safe and sound!

The crowd of bystanders cheered along with Sarah, Blaire and Cody. They went and got their bikes where they had left them. Looking at each other in a confused manner, the friends couldn't decide what to do next. Cody grinned and said, "Enough excitement today, let's just go riding!"

13. What detail shows the emotions of the characters once the baby calf was safe? Circle the correct answer choice.

Ⓐ The crowd of bystanders cheered along with Sarah, Blaire and Cody.
Ⓑ "What is going on?" asked Sarah.
Ⓒ Cody grinned and said, "Enough excitement today, let's just go riding!"
Ⓓ None of the above.

Question 14 is based on the story below

Excerpt from Jo's Boys
Chapter 1 - Ten Years Later
by Louisa May Alcott

"If anyone had told me what wonderful changes were to take place here in ten years, I wouldn't have believed it." said Mrs. Jo to Mrs. Meg, as they sat on the piazza at Plumfield one summer day, looking about them with faces full of pride and pleasure.

"This is the sort of magic that money and kind hearts can work. I am sure Mr. Laurence could have no nobler monument than the college he so generously endowed; and a home like this will keep Aunt March's memory green as long as it lasts". Answered Mrs. Meg, always glad to praise the absent.

"We used to believe in fairies, you remember, and plan what we'd ask for if we could have three wishes. Doesn't it seem as if mine had been really granted at last? Money, fame, and plenty of the work I love," said Mrs. Jo, carelessly rumpling up her hair as she clasped her hands over her head just as she used to do when a girl.

"I have had mine, and Amy is enjoying hers to her heart's content. If dear Marmee, John, and Beth were here, it would be quite perfect,"added Meg, with a tender quiver in her voice; for Marmee's place was empty now.

Jo put her hand on her sister's, and both sat silent for a little while, surveying the pleasant scene before them with mingled sad and happy thoughts.

Something magical happened in a quiet place called Plumfield. Everything changed. The house became even more welcoming with fresh paint, new wings, and a beautiful garden. It looked prosperous and happy, unlike before when there were noisy boys running around and the Bhaers had a hard time making enough money. On top of the hill, where people used to fly kites, there was now a wonderful college. Students were busy walking along the paths that used to be for playing. They were getting lots of knowledge and enjoying the good things that come with wealth, wisdom, and kindness.

14. Who are the main characters in this selection? Remember main characters are those that are most important. Write a sentence explaining your answer.

Question 15 is based on the passage below

Playing Video Games

Scotty loves to play video games! I mean he plays every chance he gets. He even plays when he should be doing his homework, chores or going to bed! It has gotten so bad that his parents are considering a punishment to teach him a lesson.

Scotty doesn't understand why they are upset with him and is trying to figure out what he can do so that he doesn't get his video game machine taken away. He has asked his friends for their ideas on the subject, too. He even asked his counselor at school. Scotty has been seeing her since his grades started dropping. The counselor told him it is very simple, give up the game playing on his own and get back to doing homework, chores, and going to bed on time.

To Scotty, the ideas his counselor told him are good, but he is very reluctant to do it. So one of his friends, Hailey, has offered to help. She is going to make him a chart of time spent on playing games compared to time spent on his responsibilities. He agrees to give it a try.

The following is his chart for the first week.

	Monday	Tuesday	Wednesday	Thursday	Friday	Saturday	Sunday	Totals
Playing Video Games	4 hours	4 hours	3 hours	3 hours	2 hours	3 hours	3 hours	22 hours
Doing Home-work	30 min	30 min	1 hour	1 hour	1 hour	none	none	4 hours
Doing Chores	15 min	15 min	45 min	45 min	45 min	2 hours	1 hour	5 hours 45 min
Going to Bed On Time	Not done	Not done	Not done	Done	Not done	Done	Done	Went to bed on time 3 days

15. Has Scotty's attitude toward doing his homework and chores improved or not?

Ⓐ His attitude has not improved during the first week.
Ⓑ His attitude has shown some improvement.
Ⓒ There is no change in his behavior.

CHAPTER 1 → Lesson 6: Figurative Language Expressions

1. What is the meaning of the phrase "can't go on"?

- (A) Cannot go back
- (B) Cannot switch it on
- (C) Cannot continue
- (D) Cannot stop fighting

2. What does the underlined phrase mean in this stanza?

I quarreled with my brother
I don't know what about,
One thing led to another
And somehow we fell out.
The start of it was slight,
The end of it was strong,
He said he was right,
I knew he was wrong!
~Eleanor Farjeon

- (A) had a disagreement
- (B) fell down
- (C) fainted
- (D) were pushed out

3. What is the meaning of the word "charging up" in the following sentence?

Just as he trumpeted, he heard a loud crashing and stamping. A herd of wrinkled elephants came charging up.

- (A) walked away
- (B) walked slowly forward
- (C) came up to dance
- (D) rushed forward to attack

4. What is the meaning of the underlined phrase?

My grandfather bought two new cars and a boat last Saturday. <u>He is made of money!</u>

- Ⓐ poor
- Ⓑ rich
- Ⓒ a thief
- Ⓓ a banker

5. What is the meaning of the underlined phrase?

My little sister won't leave me alone when I try to work on my homework. She was so annoying last night that I told her to <u>take a hike</u>!

- Ⓐ go outside and take a walk in the woods
- Ⓑ go to your room
- Ⓒ go away
- Ⓓ stop talking

6. What does the underlined phrase mean?

Jonah thought I cheated when we were playing a video game against each other, but I told him <u>I won fair and square</u>.

- Ⓐ cheating
- Ⓑ dishonestly
- Ⓒ honestly
- Ⓓ in the last minute

7. What does the underlined phrase mean?

My cousin broke my aunt's favorite coffee cup. I told him, "When your mom finds out you did this, <u>you're toast</u>!"

- Ⓐ making breakfast
- Ⓑ need to lie
- Ⓒ in big trouble
- Ⓓ going to have to explain

8. What does the underlined phrase mean?

I hate to be told what to do! Whenever someone tells me how to act, I <u>dig my heels</u> in and do what I want to do!

- (A) put my feet on the floor
- (B) dig a hole
- (C) give something a try
- (D) refuse to do something

9. What does the underlined phrase in the sentence mean?

Even though it was the final inning of the baseball game and the score was tied, the batter <u>kept his cool</u> when he came up to bat. He calmly hit a home run giving his team enough runs to win the game.

- (A) drank some cold water
- (B) took a break
- (C) stayed calm
- (D) played great

Question 10 is based on the story below

Antonio walked into the house. He was feeling overwhelmed, and just didn't know what to do about his latest problem. His mom noticed his sad face and asked him to sit down. "What's that cloud hanging over your head, son?" He just shrugged. "Been a bad day?" He nodded. She pulled her son closer and said, "Tomorrow is a new day." He smiled. His mom had a way of saying these silly expressions. They never meant what he thought they did at first, but they always made him smile.

"Has that new kid been walking around with a chip on his shoulder again?"
He chuckled out loud, picturing in his mind the new student walking around with a huge concrete block or some other "chip" on his shoulder. "Guess so…."

"Don't beat around the bush with him anymore, son….just tell him how you feel."
Antonio returned his mom's hug, squeezing her as hard as he could.
"Mom, you sure do have a way with words." The two smiled happily. "What's for dinner? I could eat a horse."

10. What did Antonio's mom mean when she asked him about the cloud hanging over his head?

- (A) She wanted to know if he felt sick.
- (B) She wanted to know why he was so sad.
- (C) She wanted to know if he had any homework.
- (D) She wanted to know if it was going to rain soon.

Water! Water! Safe and clean.

Did you know that as humans, we are full of water in our bodies? Yes, we are! We do know that we must have water to stay alive. We never think about it being a problem to have plenty of water to drink, bathe, wash clothes, and do dishes or even to water our yards. In past years, many environmentalists (people who study our surroundings and who worry about our lands), have warned us that we are not taking good care of our natural resources, water being one of those. We have seen pollution in rivers, streams and wetlands. This will eventually have a negative impact on our easy access to good clean water.

So, here is the question posed to you. What can you do to help? You might think to yourself, "Me, I am just a kid!" You can help. Keep your lawns and driveways free of litter. Water your yard only every 3-5 days. Be sure to turn off water hoses immediately after use.

Volunteer to help on a weekly basis to go around and pick up litter in your town. Make a list of where you find litter the most and get your friends or class in on the project. Picking up litter will help our water to stay cleaner, too. The less litter we have the fewer possibilities for trash to enter our waterways.

Do not use plastic bottles or bags. Get your parents to use the cloth bags when they shop for groceries. If you do use plastic, be sure to recycle it. Plastic is bad for our communities and can cause multiple types of pollution.

When showering or bathing, time your shower or bath. Make a chart and have your family do the same. Not only will you save our precious water resources, but you will save your family money on the monthly water bill, as well.

When you wash clothes in the washing machine, do not overfill your water. Either wash smaller loads, or a larger load when necessary. Most washing machines have a level to help you not overuse water.

Water is one of our greatest natural resources. We need it! It is up to all of us to be responsible to keep it plentiful and clean.

11. Litter can end up in our _____ and cause pollution to our water. Select all the correct answers that fits into the sentence above.

Ⓐ rivers
Ⓑ streams
Ⓒ wetlands

12. Instead of plastic bags, get your parents to use the _____ bags when they buy groceries.

13. Water is a _____ resource.

Question 14 is based on the story below

Christopher's Magic Reading Tricks!

There are many ways to help you in understanding things you read.
Here are some examples of ways that Christopher uses to help him in his reading.

The first one is what his teacher calls prior knowledge. This means that as you read you think -what do I already know if anything about this topic? Christopher says it helps him remember if he has ever read anything about it before. Then he uses that and tries to learn something new as he reads.

The second way is to question as you read. Think to yourself- what is the author trying to tell me, before, during and after you read? Christopher likes to say- "Self, what is it I am trying to learn as I read this? Can I repeat it after I read it?"

The third and Christopher says the most fun is to make a picture in your mind while you read. He says that if it is a story, you can even make a movie in your mind! Teachers use the term visualize your reading.

The fourth strategy or technique that Christopher learned from his teacher is to infer. This one means that Christopher has to use clues in the reading to figure out what is going on or what the author really means in the story.

The most favorite way for Christopher to get more out of what he has read is to summarize the reading. He tells his friends who may be struggling with this to tell what's important in a sentence or two after you read.

Christopher likes to reread his passages or stories more than one time when he knows he is going to be tested over them or asked questions about them. He says he also takes notes and sometimes uses more than one way to help him read better.

He had a hard time with reading when he was in first and second grade, but now since he uses these "magic tricks" to reading, he loves reading!

 70

LumosLearning.com

14. Match the magic reading trick with its definition. Write the definition from Table 1 against each magic trick.

> ### Table 1
> A. Use what you already know to learn more.
> B. Tell what's important in a sentence or two.
> C. Ask yourself what is the author trying to tell me?
> D. Read the story or passage again.
> E. Make pictures or movies in your mind about the story.
> F. Use the clues in reading to figure out what is really going on.

Definition	Magic Tricks for reading
Infer	F. Use the clues in reading to figure out what is really going on.
Prior Knowledge	
Summarize	
Visualize	
Question	
Reread	

Question 15 is based on the paragraph below

NASA facts and terms

NASA, National Aeronautics and Space Administration began in 1958.This occurred one year after the Soviets launched Sputnik 1. Sputnik 1 was the first artificial satellite in the entire world. This began what was known as the "space race" between Russia and the United States. NASA has excelled in many areas of space science. The greatest is that of having manned (human) space missions.

Here is a list of those:
U.S. Manned Space Programs

- Mercury: the first U.S. program for human spaceflight
- Gemini: the first two-man crews, longer missions
- Apollo: the first spaceflights to the moon
- Skylab: a place where humans lived and worked in space for extended periods of time
- Apollo-Soyuz: first international manned spaceflight
- Space shuttle: the first reusable spacecraft
- International Space Station: an effort to create a permanent orbiting laboratory in space

The following vocabulary helps you to better understand when reading about NASA and its accomplishments. Study the vocabulary, match the vocabulary to definitions. Then fill in the blanks using the context sentences.

Aeronautics - Science dealing with the operation of aircraft.

Astronaut - A person who pilots a spacecraft or works in space; a space traveler, particularly one from the United States. For example, Alan B Shepard Jr was the commander of several NASA space missions.

Johnson Space Center - The headquarters for all U.S. manned spacecraft projects conducted by NASA; the location of the Mission Control Center for manned space flights.

Kennedy Space Center - The launch facility for all U.S. space missions that carry crews.

Launch vehicle - A powerful rocket used to launch a spacecraft or satellite into space.

NASA (National Aeronautics & Space Administration) - The government agency whose mission is to research and develop safe and meaningful ways to explore space.

Orbit - The path of a spacecraft or a heavenly body as it revolves around a planet or other body.

Space shuttle - A reusable space vehicle that takes off like a rocket and lands like an airplane.

Space station - An orbiting spacecraft designed to be occupied by teams of astronauts or cosmonauts over a long period.

15. Match the vocabulary with the definition. Write the correct definition against each of the words given.

A. headquarters of US manned spacecraft projects and location of Mission Control
B. the science of space craft operation
C. government agency in charge of space exploration
D. launch facility in Cape Canaveral, FL
E. orbiting space craft designed for occupancy for long period of time
F. a reusable space craft, takes off like a rocket, lands like a plane
G. powerful rocket used to launch space craft or satellite
H. a person who operates spacecraft or works in space, from US
I. path of a spacecraft or heavenly body as it goes around a planet

Definition	Vocabulary
NASA	C. government agency in charge of space exploration
Launch vehicle	
Aeronautics	
Astronaut	
Space shuttle	
Orbit	
Johnson Space Center	
Kennedy Space Center	
Space Station	

CHAPTER 1 → Lesson 7: Parts of a Whole

Question 1 is based on the poem below

Camels are bumpy,
Their backs are all lumpy,
Giraffes are long- legged and meek:
Bears are so growly,
Hyenas are howly,
Dolphins are slippery and sleek.

Kangaroos have a pocket,
But no way to lock it,
Their babies can look out and peep,
But monkeys are funny
I wish I had money,
Enough to buy one and keep.

1. The above poem has two _____ .

- (A) stanzas
- (B) paragraphs
- (C) passages
- (D) parts

Question 2 is based on the paragraph below

An astronomer used to go out every night to observe stars. Often, he would be seen with a telescope in one hand and a notebook in the other. One evening, while he wandered through the suburbs with his attention fixed on the sky, he accidentally fell into a deep uncovered well. He cried out loudly for help. As he waited to be rescued, he moaned and howled about his sores and bruises. His neighbor was passing by and happened to hear his wailing and weeping. He quickly helped him out of the well. After he came to know how the accident happened, this is what he said to the astronomer: "Hark you old fellow, why in striving to pry into heaven, do you not manage to see what is on earth?"

2. What line from the paragraph tells the reader where the astronomer lived?

- (A) One evening, while he wandered through the suburbs.
- (B) He quickly helped him out of the well.
- (C) He would often be seen with a telescope in one hand and a notebook in the other.
- (D) It does not tell us where he lived.

Question 3 is based on the story below

PART II. THE FIREBRAND IN THE FOREST

When the two women saw that the wolf had the firebrand, they were very angry, and straightway they ran after him.

"Catch it and run!" cried the wolf, and he threw it to the deer. The deer caught it and ran.
"Catch it and run!" cried the deer, and he threw it to the bear. The bear caught it and ran.
"Catch it and fly!" cried the bear, and he threw it to the bat. The bat caught it and flew.
"Catch it and run!" cried the bat, and he threw it to the squirrel. The squirrel caught it and ran.

"Oh, serpent," called the two old women, "you are no friend to the First Americans. Help us. Get the firebrand away from the squirrel."

As the squirrel ran swiftly over the ground, the serpent sprang up and tried to seize the firebrand. He did not get it, but the smoke went into the squirrel's nostrils and made him cough. He would not let go of the firebrand, but ran and ran till he could throw it to the frog.

When the frog was running away with it, the squirrel for the first time thought of himself, and he found that his beautiful bushy tail was no longer straight, for the fire had curled it up over his back.

"Do not be sorry," called the young First American across the pond. "Whenever a First American boy sees a squirrel with his tail curled up over his back, he will throw him a nut."

PART III. THE FIREBRAND IN THE POND

All this time the firebrand was burning, and the frog was going to the pond as fast as he could. The old women were running after him, and when he came to the water, one of them caught him by the tail.

"I have caught him!" she called.
"Do not let him go!" cried the other.

"No, I will not," said the first; but she did let him go, for the little frog tore himself away and dived into the water. His tail was still in the woman's hand, but the firebrand was safe, and he made his way swiftly across the pond.

"Here it is," said the frog.
"Where?" asked the young First American. Then the frog coughed, and out of his mouth came the firebrand. It was small, for it had been burning all this time, but it set fire to the leaves and twigs, and soon the First Americans were warm again. They sang and they danced about the flames.

This is from the work *How Fire Was Brought to the First Americans* by Cyrus MacMillian.

3. What are the bold parts of this selection called?

Ⓐ   titles
Ⓑ   parts
Ⓒ   headings
Ⓓ   topics

Question 4-6 are based on the story below

My First Trip to the Beach

About three weeks ago, Jeremiah's parents surprised him with some news. They were taking him to the beach. He was excited and couldn't wait to tell all of his friends at school.

Soon enough, Friday afternoon arrived. Jeremiah, his sister, his parents, and his nanny all loaded into the car, and set out for the long drive to Destin, Florida. Listening to DVD's grew old rather quickly. A nap was sure to allow Jeremiah to get closer to Florida without growing bored from the ride.

When he awoke from his nap, it was time to stop for dinner. He exited the car, excited to stretch his legs. "Come on, Jeremiah," exclaimed his nanny. He was glad that she had been able to come to the beach. This was also going to be her first time seeing the ocean.

After a quick meal at a fast-food restaurant, the family piled back into the car.

The family arrived at their condo, almost too tired to enjoy the peaceful sound of the ocean. As Jeremiah headed to bed, he knew that the beach would be his to explore in a few hours. He stretched out his small frame across the twin-sized bed and soon fell asleep. He awoke a few hours later, hearing his dad outside on the balcony.

When Jeremiah finally saw the view in the daylight, he was in awe. Beautiful green waters lay off in the distance. They seemed to go on and on, as far as his eyes could see. The sand reminded him of snow.

"Wanna go for a walk?" asked his dad.
Jeremiah smiled, "Yes!" Running back inside, he threw his shoes on. His dad said that he didn't want to try to wear those in the soft, grainy sand. He dressed, and then off they went.

"What's this?" asked Jeremiah, pointing to a loose mound of sand.
"This is a sand dune, it keeps the buildings safe," his dad replied.

"Oh, okay…" Jeremiah and his dad walked along the ocean's edge. There were few words spoken, but the looks on their faces expressed feelings of happiness, as they walked along the beautiful water's edge.

4. Why did Jeremiah NOT wear shoes to the beach?

Ⓐ His dad told him that they would get lost in the ocean.
Ⓑ His dad advised him against trying to walk through the sand with shoes on.
Ⓒ His mom told him that she did not want them to get dirty.
Ⓓ He had forgotten to pack shoes for the beach.

5. Why were the sand dunes located on the beach, according to Jeremiah's dad?

Ⓐ They were there to keep people from walking on the beach.
Ⓑ They were there to protect the buildings from the ocean's water.
Ⓒ Some other kids on the beach had built a huge sand mound.
Ⓓ They did not see sand dunes, except in pictures.

6. Why did the family have a quick fast-food meal?

Ⓐ They were ready to get back home.
Ⓑ They were not very hungry.
Ⓒ They wanted to save time, so they could get to the beach sooner.
Ⓓ It was the only restaurant that they could find open.

Question 7 is based on the story below

Amber entered the small grocery store. She looked at the list that her mom had sent with her. She knew that she only had enough money to buy the milk, bread, and eggs that were on the list. Quickly, she grabbed the items and paid for them.

Eying the candy on her way out, she picked up a pack of gum, looked around and saw that no one was watching her. It had been weeks since she had chewed gum, and she thought that it would be okay. She had walked a long way to the store and felt that she deserved a little treat.

Amber walked through the double doors staring at the bright green package of chewing gum in her hand. She immediately turned back around, walked back inside, and returned the gum to its spot on the display stand. The cashier smiled and nodded, but did not say a word.

7. Why did Amber put the gum back on the shelf?

Ⓐ Amber realized that she should not steal it.
Ⓑ The cashier told her that she was going to have to return it.
Ⓒ Her mom made her return it.
Ⓓ The police were watching her.

Dear Diary,

I just returned from my first trip to the beach. It was different than I expected. The water scared me a bit, but I tried to act cool in front of my little sister. I couldn't let her know how much the crashing waves scared me.

Building sand castles in the sparkling white grains of sand was a blast, and I even had a chance to bury my sister. This is every brother's dream, right? Well, not really, and she was able to break free from the sand wall that I had built around her.

My favorite place wasn't at beach, it was sitting on the balcony. I loved looking down at the emerald green waters. Maybe when we do go back again, I won't be afraid to wander out a little farther into the water. Dad seemed to enjoy it a lot. Mom was a lot like me. She just wanted to stay close to the shore.

Jeremiah

P. S. Oh, I almost forgot to tell you that we went looking for crabs three nights in a row, but we did not have any luck. It was still fun. My fear of the ocean seemed to disappear in the night.

8. What was one thing that made Jeremiah really enjoy his visit to the beach?

   Ⓐ   Finding a lot of crabs in his evening walks on the beach.
   Ⓑ   Building sand castles and burying his sister in the sand.
   Ⓒ   Swimming in the ocean.
   Ⓓ   Tearing down the sand dunes that were built near the condo.

BROCK: (Brock enters the stage.) What a great day it is.
TERRY: (Snarls)What's good about it?
BROCK: (Laughs) I found something outside on the playground.
TERRY: (Rolls eyes).
MRS. ADAMS: (Walks over). Good morning, boys.
BROCK AND TERRY: Good morning.
MRS. ADAMS: (MOTIONS). Sit down, boys.
TERRY: (Pushes Brock.)
BROCK: Why'd you do that? (In a rather loud voice).
TERRY: (Throws hands into the air and pushes Brock again).
MRS. ADAMS: (Runs over). Boys, is this how we want to start off the week?
TERRY: (Sighs.) But, Brock says it is a great day, and…

MRS. ADAMS: (Looks confused). You are upset, just because Brock is happy?
TERRY: (Shakes head no).
BROCK: I don't know what's wrong with him.
TERRY: (Reaches into his pocket.) My mom gave me twenty dollars to pay for my lunch bill, but I can't find it. She is going to be really mad.
BROCK: (Smiles)
MRS. ADAMS: When did you last have the money?
BROCK: (Reaches into his pocket.) Remember that I told you I found something?
TERRY: (Nods).
BROCK: (Hands money to Terry). I found this outside. I bet you dropped it.
TERRY: (Hugs Brock).

9. What made Terry act so mean towards his friend, Brock?

(A) He lost the money that he needed to pay his lunch bill.
(B) Brock said something mean to him at recess.
(C) Brock stole Terry's lunch money.
(D) Terry wasn't feeling good and wanted to get in trouble, so the school would send him home.

Question 10 is based on the story below

Jasmine nervously left the car. She and her parents had been riding for what seemed like days, but after ten hours, they were finally here. She carefully studied the old farmhouse. "Are you ready?" her dad asked. Jasmine only shrugged. She had talked with her "G", as the kind lady had referred to herself, a few times on the phone, but at the age of eight, she had never actually met her grandma. It seemed that work, school, or illness had kept her away.

Jasmine's parents had told her stories about her "G" and that she had met her when she was only a few months old, but in Jasmine's mind this was the first time. She exited the car and was greeted by a petite, black-haired lady, standing in the doorway. Her smile looked familiar. It seemed to be a combination of her own and the warm smile that her dad seldom showed, but that warmed her heart, over and over.

Her "G" had scooped her up. "Come on in here, Jasmine." Jasmine felt a bit nervous, but she walked into the house with her grandmother's arms still around her. I bet you are tired of sitting. "How long have you had my beautiful granddaughter cooped up in that car?" asked her "G".
Jasmine's dad replied, "It has been a while."

"Come on, honey. There is so much that I want to show you," her grandma cooed. Jasmine followed her grandmother through the house. It seemed that they exited one doorway, only to enter another. "Here is a surprise for you," her grandma stated. Looking down, Jasmine saw the most beautiful locket. She picked it up, nervously. "I have been saving this for you. It was your great granny's...my mom's." Jasmine pulled it closer for a better view.
"Let me put it on you, you beautiful girl."

10. Why did Jasmine's "G" wait so long to give her the locket?

Ⓐ G's own mom had given her permission to give it to Jasmine.
Ⓑ It was the first time that they had ever met.
Ⓒ She had misplaced the locket and finally found it, so she was able to pass it on to Jasmine.
Ⓓ It was the first time that she had seen her granddaughter who was now old enough to understand the specialty of a locket.

Question 11 is based on the story below

OLD-FASHIONED FAIRY TALES
By Juliana Horatia Gatty Ewing

The following fairy tale is separated into 4 parts. Each part has questions that go along with the section, to help the reader have a better understanding of the tale. Also, for the reader, the selection has been numbered. Remember to read the selections more than one time for comprehension purposes.

While reading this fairy tale, keep in mind that it is written in what is called Old English. This means some words are used or spelled differently than the vocabulary we use today. Should you have difficulty with the words, use context clues to help. You may also ask your teacher, or use a dictionary to help you understand the meaning.

GOOD LUCK IS BETTER THAN GOLD.

Part 1

1. There was once upon a time a child who had Good Luck for his godfather.

2. "I am not Fortune," said Good Luck to the parents; "I have no gifts to bestow, but whenever he needs help I will be at hand."
3. "Nothing could be better," said the old couple. They were delighted. But what pleases the father often fails to satisfy the son: moreover, every man thinks that he deserves just a little more than he has got, and does not reckon it to the purpose if his father had less.

4. Many a one would be thankful to have as good reasons for contentment as he who had Good Luck for his godfather.

5. If he fell, Good Luck popped something soft in the way to break his fall; if he fought, Good Luck directed his blows, or tripped up his adversary; if he got into a scrape, Good Luck helped him out of it; and if ever Misfortune met him, Good Luck contrived to hustle her on the pathway till his godson got safely by.

6. In games of hazard the godfather played over his shoulder. In matters of choice he chose for him. And when the lad began to work on his father's farm the farmer began to get rich. For no bird or field-mouse touched a seed that his son had sown, and every plant he planted throve when Good

Luck smiled on it.

7. The boy was not fond of work, but when he did go into the fields, Good Luck followed him.

8. "Your christening-day was a blessed day for us all," said the old farmer.

9. "He has never given me so much as a lucky sixpence," muttered Good Luck's godson.

10. "I am not Fortune—I make no presents," said the godfather.

11. When we are discontented, it is oftener to please our neighbours than ourselves. It was because the other boys had said—"Simon, the shoemaker's son, has an alderman for his godfather. He gave him a silver spoon with the Apostle Peter for the handle; but thy godfather is more powerful than any alderman"—that Good Luck's godson complained, "He has never given me so much as a bent sixpence."

Part 2

12. By and by the old farmer died, and his son grew up, and had the largest farm in the country. The other boys grew up also, and as they looked over the farmer's boundary-wall, they would say:

13. "Good-morning, Neighbor. That is certainly a fine farm of yours. Your cattle thrive without loss. Your crops grow in the rain and are reaped with the sunshine. Mischance never comes to your road. What you have worked for you enjoy. Such success would turn the heads of poor folk like us. At the same time, one would think a man need hardly work for his living at all who has Good Luck for his godfather."

14. "That is very true," thought the farmer. "Many a man is prosperous, and reaps what he sows, who had no more than the clerk and the sexton for gossips at his christening."

15. "What is the matter, Godson?" asked Good Luck, who was with him in the field.

16. "I want to be rich," said the farmer.

17. "You will not have to wait long," replied the godfather. "In every field you sow, in every flock you rear there is increase without abatement. Your wealth is already tenfold greater than your father's."

18. "Aye, aye," replied the farmer. "Good wages for good work. But many a young man has gold at his command who need never turn a sod, and none of the Good People came to his christening. Fortunatus's Purse now, or even a sack or two of gold—"

19. "Peace!" cried the godfather; "I have said that I give no gifts."

20. Though he had not Fortunatus's Purse, the farmer had money and to spare, and when the harvest was gathered in, he bought a fine suit of clothes, and took his best horse and went to the royal city to see the sights.

21. The pomp and splendour, the festivities and fine clothes dazzled him.

22. "This is a gay life which these young courtiers lead," said he. "A man has nothing to do but to enjoy himself."

23. "If he has plenty of gold in his pocket," said a bystander.

24. By and by the Princess passed in her carriage. She was the King's only daughter. She had hair made of sunshine, and her eyes were stars.

25. "What an exquisite creature!" cried the farmer. "What would not one give to possess her?"

26. "She has as many suitors as hairs on her head," replied the bystander. "She wants to marry the Prince of Moonshine, but he only dresses in silver, and the King thinks he might find a richer son-in-law. The Princess will go to the highest bidder."

27. "And I have Good Luck for my godfather, and am not even at court!" cried the farmer; and he put spurs to his horse, and rode home.

Part 3

28. Good Luck was taking care of the farm.

29. "Listen, Godfather!" cried the young man. "I am in love with the King's daughter, and would want her to wife."

30. "It is not an easy matter," replied Good Luck, "but I will do what I can for you. Say that by good luck you saved the Princess's life, or perhaps better the King's—for they say he is selfish—"

31. "Tush!" cried the farmer. "The King is covetous, and wants a rich son-in-law."

32. "A wise man may bring wealth to a kingdom with his head, if not with his hands," said Good Luck, "and I can show you a district where the earth only wants mining to be flooded with wealth. Besides, there are a thousand opportunities that can be turned to account and influence. By wits and work, and with Good Luck to help him, many a poorer man than you has risen to greatness."

33. "Wits and work!" cried the indignant godson. "You speak well—truly! A hillman would have made a better godfather. Give me as much gold as will fill three meal-bins, and you may keep the rest of your help for those who want it."

34. Now at this moment by Good Luck stood Dame Fortune. She likes handsome young men, and there was some little jealousy between her and the godfather so she smiled at the quarrel.

35. "You would rather have had me for your gossip?" said she.

36. "If you would give me three wishes, I would," replied the farmer boldly, "and I would trouble you no more."

37. "Will you make him over to me?" said Dame Fortune to the godfather.

38. "If he wishes it," replied Good Luck. "But if he accepts your gifts, he has no further claim on me."

39. "Nor on me either," said the Dame. "Hark ye, young man, you mortals are apt to make a hobble of your three wishes, and you may end with a sausage at your nose, like your betters."

40. "I have thought of it too often," replied the farmer, "and I know what I want. For my first wish I desire imperishable beauty."

41. "It is yours," said Dame Fortune, smiling as she looked at him.

42. "The face of a prince and the manners of a clown are poor partners," said the farmer. "My second wish is for suitable learning and courtly manners, which cannot be gained at the plough-tail."

43. "You have them in perfection," said the Dame, as the young man thanked her by a graceful bow.

44. "Thirdly," said he, "I demand a store of gold that I can never exhaust."

45. "I will lead you to it," said Dame Fortune; and the young man was so eager to follow her that he did not even look back to bid farewell to his godfather.

Part 4

46. He was soon at court. He lived in the utmost pomp. He had a suit of armor made for himself out of beaten gold. No metal less precious might come near his person, except for the blade of his sword. This was obliged to be made of steel, for gold is not always strong enough to defend one's life or his honour. But the Princess still loved the Prince of Moonshine.

47. "Stuff and nonsense!" said the King. "I shall give you to the Prince of Gold."

48. "I wish I had the good luck to please her," muttered the young Prince. But he had not, for all his beauty and his wealth. However, she was to marry him, and that was something.

49. The preparations for the wedding were magnificent.

50. "It is a great expense," sighed the King, "but then I get the Prince of Gold for a son-in-law."

51. The Prince and his bride drove around the city in a triumphal procession. Her hair fell over her like sunshine, but the starlight of her eyes was cold.

52. In the train rode the Prince of Moonshine, dressed in silver, and with no color in his face.

53. As the bridal chariot approached one of the city gates, two black ravens hovered over it, and then flew away, and settled on a tree.

54. Good Luck was sitting under the tree to see his godson's triumph, and he heard the birds talking above him.

55. "Has the Prince of Gold no friend who can tell him that there is a loose stone above the archway that is tottering to fall?" said they. And Good Luck covered his face with his mantle as the Prince drove through.

56. Just as they were passing out of the gateway the stone fell on to the Prince's head. He wore a casque of pure gold, but his neck was broken.

57. "We can't have all this expense for nothing," said the King: so he married his daughter to the Prince of Moonshine. If one can't get gold, one must be content with silver.

58. "Will you come to the funeral?" asked Dame Fortune of the godfather.

59. "Not I," replied Good Luck. "I had no hand in this matter."
60. The rain came down in torrents. The black feathers on the ravens' backs looked as if they had been oiled.
61. "Caw! caw!" said they. "It was an unlucky end."

11. Part A
What happened to the Prince of Gold at the end?

Part B
Write a sentence explaining why this happened.

Question 12 is based on the poem below

FOREIGN LANDS

Up into the cherry tree
Who should climb but little me?
I held the trunk with both my hands
And looked abroad on foreign lands.

I saw the next-door garden lie,
Adorned with flowers, before my eye,
And many pleasant faces more
That I had never seen before.

I saw the dimpling river pass
And be the sky's blue looking-glass;
The dusty roads go up and down
With people tramping into town.
If I could find a higher tree

Farther and farther I should see,
To where the grown-up river slips
Into the sea among the ships.

To where the roads on either hand
Lead onward into fairyland,
Where all the children dine at five,
And all the playthings come alive.

-- By Robert Louis Stevenson

12. In your own words, explain the rhyming pattern that the poet Robert Louis Stevenson uses in this poem.

Question 13 is based on the story below

CHAPTER I: Looking-Glass House
Excerpt taken from Alice in Wonderland, Through the Looking Glass

One thing was certain, that the white kitten had nothing to do with it:—it was the black kitten's fault entirely. For the white kitten had been having its face washed by the old cat for the last quarter of an hour (and bearing it pretty well, considering); so you see that it couldn't have had any hand in the mischief.

The way Dinah washed her children's faces was this: first she held the poor thing down by its ear with one paw, and then with the other paw she rubbed its face all over, the wrong way, beginning at the nose: and just now, as I said, she was hard at work on the white kitten, which was lying quite still and trying to purr—no doubt feeling that it was all meant for its good.

But the black kitten had been finished with earlier in the afternoon, and so, while Alice was sitting curled up in a corner of the great arm-chair, half talking to herself and half asleep, the kitten had been having a grand game of romps with the ball of worsted Alice had been trying to wind up, and had been rolling it up and down till it had all come undone again; and there it was, spread over the hearth-rug, all knots and tangles, with the kitten running after its own tail in the middle.
'Oh, you wicked little thing!' cried Alice, catching up the kitten, and giving it a little kiss to make

it understand that it was in disgrace. 'Really, Dinah ought to have taught you better manners! You ought, Dinah, you know you ought!' she added, looking reproachfully at the old cat, and speaking in as cross a voice as she could manage—and then she scrambled back into the arm-chair, taking the kitten and the worsted with her, and began winding up the ball again. But she didn't get on very fast, as she was talking all the time, sometimes to the kitten, and sometimes to herself. Kitty sat very demurely on her knee, pretending to watch the progress of the winding, and now and then putting out one paw and gently touching the ball, as if it would be glad to help, if it might.

'Do you know what to-morrow is, Kitty?' Alice began. 'You'd have guessed if you'd been up in the window with me—only Dinah was making you tidy, so you couldn't. I was watching the boys getting in sticks for the bonfire—and it wants plenty of sticks, Kitty! Only it got so cold, and it snowed so, they had to leave off. Never mind, Kitty, we'll go and see the bonfire to-morrow.' Here Alice wound two or three turns of the worsted round the kitten's neck, just to see how it would look: this led to a scramble, in which the ball rolled down upon the floor, and yards and yards of it got unwound

13. By using the details in the story, what do you think is the setting of the story? Write a sentence that supports your answer.

___

Question 14 is based on the story below

The Adventures of Huckleberry Finn by Mark Twain

Excerpt- public domain

I wanted to go and look at a place right about the middle of the island that I'd found when I was exploring; so we started and soon got to it, because the island was only three miles long and a quarter of a mile wide.

This place was a tolerable long, steep hill or ridge about forty feet high. We had a rough time getting to the top, the sides were so steep and the bushes so thick. We tramped and clumb around all over it, and by and by found a good big cavern in the rock, most up to the top on the side towards Illinois. The cavern was as big as two or three rooms bunched together, and Jim could stand up straight in it. It was cool in there. Jim was for putting our traps in there right away, but I said we didn't want to be climbing up and down there all the time.

Jim said if we had the canoe hid in a good place, and had all the traps in the cavern, we could rush there if anybody was to come to the island, and they would never find us without dogs. And, besides, he said them little birds had said it was going to rain, and did I want the things to get wet?

So, we went back, and got the canoe, and paddled up abreast the cavern, and lugged all the traps up there. Then we hunted up a place close by to hide the canoe in, amongst the thick willows. We took some fish off of the lines and set them again, and begun to get ready for dinner.

The door of the cavern was big enough to roll a hogshead in, and on one side of the door the floor stuck out a little bit, and was flat and a good place to build a fire on. So we built it there and cooked dinner.

14. **In this excerpt from Huckleberry Finn, where does the setting of the story take place? Circle the correct answer choice.**

   Ⓐ The setting is in Huck's backyard.
   Ⓑ The setting is on a grassy hillside.
   Ⓒ The setting is on an island in a cavern.
   Ⓓ None of the above.

Question 15 is based on the poem below

"A Little Road Not Made Of Man"
By Emily Elizabeth Dickinson

A little road not made of man,
Enabled of the eye,
Accessible to thill of bee,
Or cart of butterfly.

If town it have, beyond itself,
'T is that I cannot say;
I only sigh, -- no vehicle
Bears me along that way.

15. **Which are the correct rhyming words in patterns from the poem? Circle the correct answer choice.**

   Ⓐ man, can, eye, bee.
   Ⓑ eye, butterfly, say, way.
   Ⓒ butterfly, sigh, eye, way.
   Ⓓ road, cart, eye, butterfly.

CHAPTER 1 → Lesson 8: Who's Talking Now?

Question 1 is based on the poem below

I had a silver buckle,
I sewed it on my shoe,
And 'neath a sprig of mistletoe
I danced the evening through!
I had a bunch of cowslips,
I hid 'em in a grot,
In case the elves should come by night
And me remember not.
I had a yellow ribbon,
I tied it in my hair,
That, walking in the garden,
The birds might see it there.
I had a secret laughter,
I laughed it near the wall:
Only the ivy and the wind
May tell of it at all.

By Walter de la Mare (1873-1956), under the pseudonym Walter Ramal, title unknown, from Songs of Childhood, published 1902.

1. Who is the narrator of this poem?

Ⓐ   the birds
Ⓑ   an elf
Ⓒ   I (the writer, author)
Ⓓ   the ivy

Question 2 is based on the paragraph below

Pearl reached in her pocket for the coins, but she could not feel them. Desperately, she pulled everything out of her pocket. She found a chocolate wrapper, a bus pass, her student ID card, lipstick, mascara, and her cell phone. There were NO coins!

2. Who is telling this story about Pearl?

- Ⓐ Pearl
- Ⓑ Pearl's mother
- Ⓒ a narrator
- Ⓓ the bus driver

Question 3 is based on the poem below

The Goose that Laid the Golden Egg

A man once had a goose I'm told,
Which had laid each day an egg of gold.
Now if this treasure were well spent,
It might make any one content.
But no! This man desired more;
And though of eggs he had rich store;
He thought one day the goose he'd kill,

And then at once his pockets fill.
So chasing goosey round and round,
She soon was caught and firmly bound
He opened her from neck to tail
And then his folly did bewail.
For not a single egg was there,
And thus he lost this treasure rare.

3. Who is telling the story in this poem? Mark "Yes" or "No" against each character.

	Yes	No
The man	○	○
The goose	○	○
A narrator, outside of the story	○	○
The golden eggs	○	○

I Don't Want To Go

Emily zipped up her suitcase, sighed loudly, and then lugged it out to the Family Utility Vehicle. "Why do I have to go?" she asked.

"This is a family vacation," replied her dad.

Sure it was, she thought. The idea of spending three entire days and nights sleeping in a tent out in the wilderness that was named after the explorer Daniel Boone did not appeal to her girly side. "Mom, can we stay...?"

Before she could finish, Emily's younger brother came bolting out the door, his suitcase overflowing, and his momentum almost knocking her to the ground. "Let's go, let's go."

Emily climbed into the backseat, her MP3 player blasting loudly; at least she had some piece of civilization left. As they drove for what seemed like forever, Emily enjoyed peering out the window. As they got farther and farther away from the city, she began to catch glimpses of rabbits, squirrels, and various birds that she wasn't used to seeing. The tall buildings and annoying noises of the city began to be replaced by a peaceful quiet. She turned her music off, but kept the ear buds in place, as she didn't want anyone to know that she was enjoying the ride. Finally, she saw the sign: Welcome to the Daniel Boone National Forest.

"Can we hike to the falls?" her brother asked.

She exited the vehicle, declared that she was ready for a walk. She had heard about Cumberland Falls but had never actually seen them. Some of her classmates had mentioned that they were smaller, but a lot like Niagara Falls. She had no desire to let the others know she was excited, but she hoped that her dad would say that they could go exploring.

Looking around her, she saw huge mountains that seemed to tower above the river below. This was much different from the small subdivision that she called home. Just maybe the next three days wouldn't be so bad. As she removed her earbuds, she smiled, as a small deer crossed the pathway several hundred feet in the distance. The first live deer that she had ever seen was when she was twelve. " Wow, this is really amazing! Let's take that walk, Dad."

"Really?" he asked.

4. What point of view is this story written in?

Ⓐ First person spoken through Emily's voice.
Ⓑ First person spoken through Emily's dad's voice.
Ⓒ Third person spoken through an outside narrator.
Ⓓ First person spoken through Emily's brother's voice.

Question 5 is based on the paragraph below

May 24, 2012
Dear Diary,

I just returned from my first trip to the beach. It was different than I expected. The water scared me a bit, but I tried to act cool in front of my little sister. I couldn't let her know how much the crashing waves scared me.

Building sand castles in the sparkling white grains of sand was a blast, and I even had a chance to bury my sister. That has to be every brother's dream, right? Well, not really, and she was able to break free from the sand wall that I had built up around her.

My favorite place wasn't at the beach, but sitting in the balcony. I loved looking down at the emerald green waters. Maybe when we go back again, I won't be afraid to wander out a little farther into the water. Dad sure did seem to enjoy that a lot. Mom was a lot like me. She just wanted to stay close to the shore.

Jeremiah

P. S. Oh, I almost forgot to tell you that we went looking for crabs three nights in a row, but we did not have any luck. It was still fun. My fear of the ocean seemed to disappear in the night.

5. From what point of view is this story presented?

- Ⓐ Jeremiah's point of view (first person)
- Ⓑ Dad's point of view (first person)
- Ⓒ Narrator point of view (third person)
- Ⓓ Mom's point of view (first person)

Question 6 is based on the story below

Danny had always been a different kind of child, so I wasn't real happy when Xavier started hanging out with him. I didn't really know how to handle the situation, but I didn't want to be one of those parents that told him he had to stop. When Xavier told me about playing with Danny that first day at recess, I remember thinking, "Oh no..."

It has been about a month since that day, and I still ask every afternoon if anyone lost recess today. It is my way of finding out if Danny or Xavier got into any trouble. This way it doesn't seem so much like I am pointing the finger at Danny. Those first few times that I asked, it seemed that Xavier was always telling me something silly that Danny did to get in trouble: spit wads, pouring his milk into another student's mashed potatoes, running in the hallway, etc. Not bad things, just things that showed disrespect. As the days passed, either Xavier has realized that I am fed up with Danny's silliness or he isn't getting in trouble as much.

I have agreed to let Danny spend the night tonight. The boys are excited about sleeping outside in the tent, and I have arranged for them to make S'mores, have a small campfire, and enjoy the comforts of almost being alone in the wilderness. "Mom, where are you? This is Danny." I stare at Danny. He looks sweet enough. His short haircut makes him look much younger than his age of eight, well, assuming that he is the same age as Xavier.

"Hi, Mrs."
"Just call me Ann. Danny, do you want to see Xavier's room?" I asked.

Danny smiled at me and I was hooked. His crystal blue eyes lit up, and his left cheek had a small, but noticeable dimple. I patted Danny on the back. "We are glad you came to visit," I stated. I walked the boys down the hallway to Xavier's room.

"What's this?" Xavier asked.
"Since this is your first official camp out, I thought you needed the right pajamas. I just guessed your size, Danny, let's hope they fit." Danny scooped the pajamas up, while Xavier just shrugged.

"Is this the bathroom?" I nodded. Moments later, Danny returned, wearing his new pajamas. They were a little large, but they would do. The boy that I had pegged to be the troublemaker seemed so sweet. He threw his tiny arms around me. "These are great…" said Danny. I could see the tears in his eyes, and I pulled him even closer.

"I am glad you like them, Danny," I stated.

6. From what point of view is this story presented?

Ⓐ   Danny's point of view (first person)
Ⓑ   Xavier's point of view (first person)
Ⓒ   Narrator's point of view (third person)
Ⓓ   Ann's point of view (first person)

Question 7 is based on the paragraph below

I am not feeling good about this at all. I had so much homework last night that I couldn't study for my science test. My stomach is tied in knots, tighter than the ones on my shoestrings. Maybe it won't be as bad as I expect. I mean, let's face it, science is science! I listen in class, I do all of my home-work assignments, and I participate in the review games. It will be okay. I am not going to panic! I am not going to panic!

7. From what point of view is this story presented?

Ⓐ   Student's point of view (first person)
Ⓑ   Parent's point of view (first person)
Ⓒ   Teacher's point of view (first person)
Ⓓ   Other's point of view (third person)

Question 8 is based on the paragraph below

An astronomer used to go out every night to observe stars. Often, he would be seen with a telescope in one hand and a notebook in the other. One evening, while he wandered through the suburbs with his attention fixed on the sky, he accidentally fell into a deep uncovered well. He cried out loudly for help. As he waited to be rescued, he moaned and howled about his sores and bruises. His neighbor was passing by and happened to hear his wailing and weeping. He quickly helped him out of the well. After he came to know how the accident happened, this is what he said to the astronomer: "Hark you old fellow, why in striving to pry into heaven, do you not manage to see what is on earth?"

8. Who is telling this story?

Ⓐ   someone outside of the story
Ⓑ   the astronomer
Ⓒ   the astronomer's wife
Ⓓ   the neighbor

Question 9 is based on the story below

Robert Bruce, King of Scotland, was hiding in a hut in the forest. His enemies were seeking him far and wide. Six times he had met them in battle, and six times he had failed. Hope and courage were gone. Bruce had given up all as lost. He was about to run away from Scotland and to leave the country in the hands of his enemies.

Full of sorrow, he lay stretched on a pile of straw in the poor woodchopper's hut. While he lay there thinking, he noticed a spider spinning her web.

The spider was trying to spin a thread from one beam of the cottage to another. It was a long way between the beams, and Bruce saw how hard a task it was for her to do. "She will never do it," thought the king. The little spider tried it once and failed. She tried it twice and failed. The king counted each attempt.

She had tried it six times and had failed each time.
"She is like me," thought the king. "I have tried six battles and failed. She has tried to reach the beam six times and failed."

Then staring up from the straw, he cried, "I will hang my fate upon the little spider. If she swings the seventh time and fails, then I will give up all for lost. If she swings the seventh time and wins, I will call my men together once more for a battle with the enemy and never give up, much like the little spider."

The spider tried the seventh time, letting herself down upon her slender thread. She swung out bravely. "Look! look!" shouted the king. "She has reached it. The thread hangs between the two beams. If the spider can do it, I can do it."

Bruce got up from the straw with new strength and sent his men from village to village, calling the people to arms. The brave soldiers answered his call and came trooping in. At length, his army was ready to fight, and when the king led them in a great battle against the enemy, this time, like the spider, Bruce won.

This is an excerpt taken from 'The Beacon Second Reader' which was written by James Fassett.

9. How would this story be different if the spider was telling the story?

Ⓐ   Robert Bruce would not be talking.
Ⓑ   The reader would hear the spider's thoughts.
Ⓒ   The spider would have given up trying to make its web.
Ⓓ   The spider's web would have been larger.

Question 10 is based on the story below

Gerry walked around enjoying nature. This was his favorite time of day. In less than an hour, the activity would slow down as the zoo closed for the day. The visitors would go home and the zoo workers would spend extra time with the animals. Many times, the workers would offer special treats. Before this could happen, Gerry had to make it through until closing. Looking up, he spotted a family walking close to the edge of the enclosure.

"Let's see the giraffe, Grandma!" one of the two little boys shouted loudly. "I want to see him," the other one yelled. "If you are not quiet, you will scare him off," the grandmother cautioned. She reached into her basket to pull out a handful of lettuce. Gerry couldn't help but move a little closer. It was his favorite kind of lettuce.

The first boy whispered quietly. "Can I have some lettuce? He is coming this way." After getting a handful of the green vegetable, the boy held it over the edge of the enclosure. "Here he comes."

Gerry closed his eyes and chewed the delicious treat in pleasure. This was definitely his favorite time of day.

10. Who is the narrator of the story?

Ⓐ The narrator is the giraffe.
Ⓑ The narrator is the grandma with a basket.
Ⓒ The narrator is NOT a character in the story.
Ⓓ The narrator is another animal that lives in the forest.

Water! Water! Safe and clean.

Did you know that as humans, we are full of water in our bodies? Yes, we are! We do know that we must have water to stay alive. We never think about it being a problem to have plenty of water to drink, bathe, wash clothes, and do dishes or even to water our yards. In past years, many environmentalists (people who study our surroundings and who worry about our lands), have warned us that we are not taking good care of our natural resources, water being one of those. We have seen pollution in rivers, streams and wetlands. This will eventually have a negative impact on our easy access to good clean water.

So, here is the question posed to you. What can you do to help? You might think to yourself, "Me, I am just a kid!" You can help. Keep your lawns and driveways free of litter. Water your yard only every 3-5 days. Be sure to turn off water hoses immediately after use.

Volunteer to help on a weekly basis to go around and pick up litter in your town. Make a list of where you find litter the most and get your friends or class in on the project. Picking up litter will help our water to stay cleaner, too. The less litter we have the fewer possibilities for trash to enter our waterways.

Do not use plastic bottles or bags. Get your parents to use the cloth bags when they shop for groceries. If you do use plastic, be sure to recycle it. Plastic is bad for our communities and can cause multiple types of pollution.

When showering or bathing, time your shower or bath. Make a chart and have your family do the same. Not only will you save our precious water resources, but you will save your family money on the monthly water bill, as well.

When you wash clothes in the washing machine, do not overfill your water. Either wash smaller loads, or a larger load when necessary. Most washing machines have a level to help you not overuse water.

Water is one of our greatest natural resources. We need it! It is up to all of us to be responsible to keep it plentiful and clean.

11. **Now, brainstorm ways that you can help to save our natural water resources. Write down your ideas below. List at least 4 ideas.**

Eating Healthy- A good start to staying strong!

Most health professionals encourage people to eat vegetables and fruit on a daily basis!

Some great vegetables include broccoli, okra, spinach, lettuce, green beans, peas, and cabbage. Try new vegetables now and then. It will help you to develop better eating habits. Who knows, you might even like them. I know when I was a kid, I was very leery of okra and spinach. Now, I love them!

Other vegetables include carrots, squash and sweet potatoes. Most kids do not like vegetables, except for carrots and green beans. Again, try a bite every now and then. Most people may not realize it, but there are some fruit like apricots, cantaloupes, and mangos that can take the place of a vegetable in your meals.

It is important in eating to pick vegetables and fruit that have been prepared with little or no added fat, sugar or salt. Fresh fruits and fresh vegetables are the best when the season is right and they are available in your area.

Most vegetables and fruit have little or no fat in them. Try to stay clear of high fat foods when you eat such as French fries, onion rings, and salads with large amounts of dressing, and/ or those fruits served with heavy creams. The same goes for fruit that is in cans or containers with heavy syrup as they have more sugar. More amounts of sugar can add unwanted calories which will make you gain weight.

Everyone knows that most kids do not buy the food, but that their parents do make those choices in stores. So next time you have a chance talk to your mom or dad or whoever does the grocery shopping. Ask them if you can go along or ask them to be sure to pick out fresh fruit whenever possible. Frozen fruit can be a good selection, too, as it is usually just packed with water.

Use your reading skills and read labels before you buy or eat. Share that information with your parents, too.

Healthy bodies need fiber found in vegetables and fruit. Juices on the other hand, do not contain the needed fiber.

Be sure to stay clear of those punches or fruit drinks that are not 100% fruit, too. Usually, they are sources of that heavy syrup and sugar additives that may taste good, but do not benefit your health.

Eating healthy is always a good choice!

12. What would be the best way to make sure you are eating healthy in regards to fruits and vegetables? Circle the correct answer choice.

Ⓐ Check your weight daily.
Ⓑ Chart what you eat on a daily basis noting if the vegetables and/or fruit were low in fat and sugar.
Ⓒ Eat tasty food and do not worry.
Ⓓ None of the above.

Who says guys only cook on the grill

My grandma, mom and sister always do the cooking in the kitchen at our house. It is very good indeed, do not get me wrong. Sometimes, however, I would like to cook on the stove, too! Dad says that guys do the grilling on the bbq pit outside. Why can't we cook inside, too?

So one day I asked Dad, "Dad, what would you like for supper tonight?" He replied, "Gee, Howard, I would really love hamburger steak with onions, but your mom doesn't want to cook that."

I announced, "Please, let me try to cook it!" Mom and Dad looked at each other and nodded yes.

I was so elated! First thing I did was ask Mom if she had everything we needed. She said she had no idea what we needed. So I looked on our computer under recipes and found several. I began to read off the ingredients. Some she had already and some she said we do not use. I decided to combine a couple of recipes and make my own. Here it is!

Ingredients for the hamburger steak patties:

1 to 1 ½ lbs of hamburger meat- preferably the ground chuck
3-4 tablespoons of cooking oil, we use canola
1 large egg
2/3 cups of really fine chopped onions
1 teaspoon of Worchester sauce- spicy sauce if you would rather
A pinch of salt
A pinch of garlic powder
A pinch of black pepper
About 1/3-1/2 cup of all-purpose flour- use that to coat the patties to brown

Now, the gravy:

Instead of making homemade gravy, Dad and I decided I could use the package of onion gravy mix- I used 2 packages!
A half of an onion sliced real thin, long slices!
A little more Worchester sauce for flavor- a splash or two

Directions:

Take the ingredients for the hamburger steak patties and mix them together- do not add the flour. Form large patties, it will probably make at least 5-6. Flatten as much as you can, but not too thin. Now pat the flour on each side of the patties. In a very large frying pan or skillet, heat your cooking oil until it starts to bubble just a bit. Now place the patties in the oil and cook on each side for about 4-5 minutes until brown. Remove them from the frying pan. Lay aside, but keep warm. (Warning, do not try to flatten your patties, as it will cause them to fall apart. One of mine did fall apart.)

While the pan is still hot and on, add the thinly sliced onions. Let them cook until they start to turn a little brown. Now, lower the flame and add the gravy mix according to the package. Turn the flame back up and let it come to a low boil. Be sure to use a spoon or ladle and stir the gravy while it is cooking.

Let the gravy mix cook on low for about 5 minutes. Add more water a little at a time if it thickens too fast. Now take the patties and add them to the gravy mix. Cover with a lid and cook for no more than 20 minutes on low.

Enjoy! We did! Yes, now my grandma, mom and sister let me cook inside any time I want to try a new recipe! Who says guys only cook on the grill?

13. Part A
   If you were to cook a meal for your family, what would you like to cook? What do you think your ingredients list might look like?

Part B
List 4 ingredients you think you might need.

Question 14 is based on the paragraph below

School Rules

The students at Morgan Lane Elementary are very upset with some of the new rules. Starting this year, they can no longer have rolling carts to carry their books, lunches, and personal items. The school board became concerned about what some kids might be hiding in the backpacks and rolling carts. Also, last spring, one of the students was hurt when another student's cart hit them in the hallway. Parents are a little upset, but they understand that for safety and security of the students and staff, this is a good idea. The new rule states that only clear see-through backpacks will be allowed. Even students' lunches have to be able to be seen.

This is not making the students happy at all. Mrs. Logan's third-graders have been talking about it all morning. Most of them had already bought their carts and colored backpacks before the rule was adopted by the school board. So here on the first day of school, they are lugging around everything. The stores ran out of the clear see-through backpacks quickly. Some parents just couldn't afford to purchase additional items at such a late date when they had already bought others before.

Needless to say all of this chatter in class, has made it rough for Mrs. Logan to teach on the first day.

She has decided to stop her lesson and have a class discussion. She is using a chart to show good reasons for the changes and to show students concerns about the changes. It also shows possible alternatives or solutions for problems that are being brought up by the students.

Here is what the chart looks like so far.

Positive Effects of New Rule	Negative Effects of New Rule	Possible Alternatives or Solutions
Fewer accidents with carts	Students who are small in size cannot carry backpacks without injury to their backs.	Put in lockers for students so they do not have to worry about carrying so much that is visible to all.
No worries about things that are unrelated to school being in backpacks	Handicap students unable to get around with backpacks	Hold an awareness session to fully explain situations behind the decision
Students and staff are better protected.	Feeling of unrest and not trusting students.	Allow small non-see through bags for personal items.

14. Give two reasons why you feel the rule is good, 2 more reasons why it is a problem and 2 more solutions. Write your answer in the box below.

CHAPTER 1 → Lesson 9: I Can See It Now

Question 1-5 are based on the graph below

Hamburgers	Corn dogs	Pizza	Spaghetti	Mac & Cheese

Look at the graph above and answer the following questions about the lunch menu at Curbside School.

1. What is the most popular item on the lunch menu?

Ⓐ Hamburgers
Ⓑ Corn dogs
Ⓒ Pizza
Ⓓ Spaghetti
Ⓔ Mac & cheese

2. What addition to the graph would make it easier for you to decide which item is liked almost as much as spaghetti?

Ⓐ Pictures
Ⓑ Headings
Ⓒ Food descriptions
Ⓓ Numbers

3. **Which item is the students' second favorite?**

   Ⓐ   Hamburgers
   Ⓑ   Corn dogs
   Ⓒ   Pizza
   Ⓓ   Spaghetti
   Ⓔ   Mac & cheese

4. **What should the lunch ladies at Curbside School serve most often to keep the students happy?**

   Ⓐ   Hamburgers
   Ⓑ   Corn dogs
   Ⓒ   Pizza
   Ⓓ   Spaghetti
   Ⓔ   Mac & cheese

5. **If the lunch ladies at Curbside School drop one item from the lunch menu, what item should be removed?**

   Ⓐ   Hamburgers
   Ⓑ   Corn dogs
   Ⓒ   Pizza
   Ⓓ   Spaghetti
   Ⓔ   Mac & cheese

6. **I think this story will be a _____. The mood will be _____. I can tell this because _____.**

   Ⓐ   A comedy, the mood will be funny, because the picture is a spaceship and spaceships are always funny.
   Ⓑ   A fantasy, the mood will be mysterious, because spaceships are intriguing.
   Ⓒ   A tragedy, the mood will be sad, because the picture is scary.
   Ⓓ   A scary tale, the mood will be frightening, because most people are scared of spaceships.

7. I think this story will be a _____. **The mood will be** _____. **I can tell this because** _____.

Ⓐ The story will be a tragedy; the mood will be sad, dogs don't like wearing hats.
Ⓑ The story will be a narrative; the mood will be happy, the dogs are smiling
Ⓒ The story will be nonfiction; the mood will be gloomy, it is a true story about a dog that is very ill.
Ⓓ The story is an autobiography; the mood will be informative, because dogs like to tell their life histories.

8. I think this story will be a _____. **The mood will be** _____. **I can tell this because** _____.

Ⓐ The story will be a comedy; the mood will be sad, because the little girl looks upset.
Ⓑ The story will be non-fiction; the mood will be funny, because the little girl is laughing.
Ⓒ The story will be a narrative; the mood will be serious, because the little girl is thinking.
Ⓓ The story will be a fantasy; the mood will be thrilling, because the little girl looks scared.

9. I think this story will be a _____. The mood will be _____. I
   can tell this because _____.

Ⓐ The story will be an autobiography; the mood will be serious, because the dragon will be
telling his life story.

Ⓑ The story will be a comedy; the mood will be funny, because the dragon looks like he likes to
tell jokes.

Ⓒ The story will be a fantasy; the mood will be scary, because the dragon looks fierce.

Ⓓ The story will be a narrative, the mood will be informational, because the imaginary creature
wants to tell the reader about dragons.

10. **What event is represented by the below logos?**

Ⓐ The Olympic games
Ⓑ A theatrical performance
Ⓒ A concert
Ⓓ A business conference

Students Likes and Dislikes

Mrs. Landry, the librarian at Happy Lane Elementary School was trying to get information about what topics her students wanted to read about. She was designing a reading plan and wanted to be sure that most of the students liked the book selections she was going to use. So, Mrs. Landry developed a chart to show the students likes and dislikes.

The following chart depicts what the third-grade students reported to her on their questionnaire form.

	Adventure	Families	Pets	Hobbies	Mystery	History
Likes	50	107	119	115	100	9
Dislikes	69	12	0	4	19	110

11. **What books should Mrs. Landry not choose to have the students read? Highlight the correct answer.**

   Ⓐ Mrs. Landry should not choose books about pets or families.
   Ⓑ Mrs. Landry should choose all the books because the students like all of them.
   Ⓒ Mrs. Landry should not choose mystery books.
   Ⓓ Mrs. Landry should not choose books about history.

States in the US

Look at the map. Then read the list of states in ABC order. Note that the states of Hawaii and Alaska are not shown in the correct location. The reason for this is simple. Alaska is located on the end of Canada far above Washington to the left. One side of Alaska is located on the Pacific Ocean. It is not connected to the rest of the US. The state of Hawaii is a group of islands located in the Pacific Ocean and again is not adjoined to the US. Thus it, too, would not fit correctly on this map. The Pacific Ocean is on the left of the map in blue, the Gulf of Mexico is on the bottom in blue and flows into the Atlantic Ocean on the right in blue.

The Fifty States in ABC Order:

Alabama, Alaska, Arizona, Arkansas, California,
Colorado, Connecticut
Delaware, Florida, Georgia, Hawaii, Idaho, Illinois,
Indiana
Iowa, Kansas, Kentucky, Louisiana, Maine,
Maryland, Massachusetts, Michigan.
Minnesota, Mississippi, Missouri, Montana,

Nebraska, Nevada,
New Hampshire, New Jersey, New Mexico, New York,
North Carolina, North Dakota, Ohio,
Oklahoma, Oregon, Pennsylvania, Rhode Island,
South Carolina,
South Dakota, Tennessee, Texas,
Utah, Vermont, Virginia, Washington, West Virginia,
Wisconsin, Wyoming.

Carefully review all that you read, and see before answering the questions below.

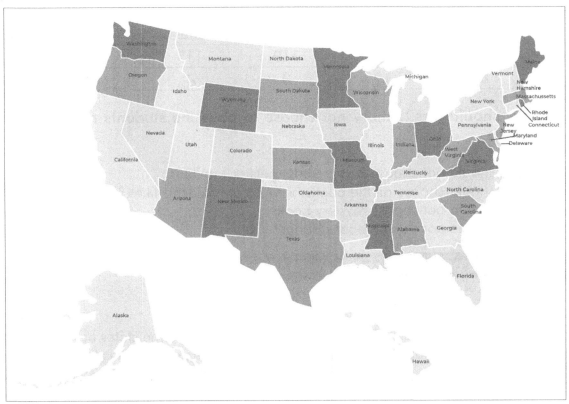

After reviewing the facts given, the map and the list of states in ABC order, answer the questions that follow.

12. Which states have the Pacific Ocean as their borders? List them. HINT: There are five.

13. Which states have the Gulf of Mexico as borders? List them.
HINT: There are 5.

Question 14 is based on the passage below

Playing Video Games

Scotty loves to play video games! I mean he plays every chance he gets. He even plays when he should be doing his homework, chores or going to bed! It has gotten so bad that his parents are considering a punishment to teach him a lesson.

Scotty doesn't understand why they are upset with him and is trying to figure out what he can do so that he doesn't get his video game machine taken away. He has asked his friends for their ideas on the subject, too. He even asked his counselor at school. Scotty has been seeing her since his grades started dropping. The counselor told him it is very simple, give up the game playing on his own and get back to doing homework, chores, and going to bed on time.

To Scotty, the ideas his counselor told him are good, but he is very reluctant to do it. So one of his friends, Hailey, has offered to help. She is going to make him a chart of time spent on playing games compared to time spent on his responsibilities. He agrees to give it a try.

14. Based on this chart, complete the chart totals. For "Going to Bed On Time", count the days he did go to bed on time.

	Monday	Tuesday	Wednesday	Thursday	Friday	Saturday	Sunday	Totals
Playing Video Games	4 hours	4 hours	3 hours	3 hours	2 hours	3 hours	3 hours	
Doing Homework	30 min	30 min	1 hour	1 hour	1 hour	none	none	
Doing Chores	15 min	15 min	45 min	45 min	45 min	2 hours	1 hour	
Going to Bed On Time	Not done	Not done	Not done	Done	Not done	Done	Done	

CHAPTER 1 → Lesson 10: Alike and Different

Question 1 and 2 are based on the story below

One day, a baby elephant was happily dancing through the jungle, nodding his head and lifting his trunk to trumpet loudly.

The loud sound woke up a monkey who was sleeping in a tree nearby. He was very angry. He scolded the elephant and asked him to keep quiet.

"You silly animal," he said. "Can't you keep quiet? I'm sleeping."

"Oh, sorry," said the little elephant, and walked on. After some time, the little elephant reached a river and saw some beautiful swans there. He gazed at the beautiful birds. The swans looked at him and began to laugh.

"Oh! Look at that big creature," they said. "What a long nose, his ears are like fans, and look at his skin, it's much too big for him. He looks like a big wrinkled bag with all of those folds!" They laughed at him and swam away.

The little elephant was very sad. He tried to smooth out his skin with his trunk, but it was no good. He thought, "Why am I so ugly? Let me hide so that no one can see me."

He tried to hide in a thick bush, but he disturbed some nests. The birds flew above his head, crying loudly while trying to peck at him.

The little elephant ran for cover. He went behind a big rock to hide. Suddenly, he saw a big bear coming towards him. It was growling and appeared to be very angry. The little elephant was very frightened and trumpeted loudly. Just as he trumpeted, he heard a loud crashing and stomping. A herd of elephants came charging to the rescue.

Seeing the herd, the frightened bear ran away.

The little elephant joyfully ran to the big elephants, thanked them, and said, "I wish I could be like you. You're so mighty and strong," he continued.

"But you are," replied the elephants. "You're a perfect little elephant." The little elephant danced for joy; he trumpeted loudly and walked away happily with the other elephants following behind.

1. **What was different about the little elephant from the other animals?**

   Ⓐ He is smaller than the other animals.
   Ⓑ He looks different than the other animals.
   Ⓒ He is weaker than the other animals.
   Ⓓ He is quieter than the other animals.

2. **Who is the little elephant most like in this story?**

   Ⓐ The other elephants
   Ⓑ The bear
   Ⓒ The birds
   Ⓓ The monkey

Question 3 is based on the paragraph below

An astronomer used to go out every night to observe stars. Often, he would be seen with a telescope in one hand and a notebook in the other. One evening, while he wandered through the suburbs with his attention fixed on the sky, he accidentally fell into a deep uncovered well. He cried out loudly for help. As he waited to be rescued, he moaned and howled about his sores and bruises. His neighbor was passing by and happened to hear his wailing and weeping. He quickly helped him out of the well. After he came to know how the accident happened, this is what he said to the astronomer: "Hark you old fellow, why in striving to pry into heaven, do you not manage to see what is on earth?"

3. **How is the neighbor different than the astronomer?**

   Ⓐ The neighbor is more interested in the sky than the astronomer is.
   Ⓑ The astronomer is awake at night while the neighbor is asleep.
   Ⓒ The astronomer likes to read, but the neighbor does not.
   Ⓓ The neighbor is concerned with things on earth while the astronomer is concerned with things in the sky.

Question 4 is based on the passages below

Read BOTH passages. Then answer the question that follows.

Passage 1 - I Don't Want To Go

Emily zipped up her suitcase, sighed loudly, and then lugged it out to the Family Utility Vehicle. "Why do I have to go?" she asked.

"This is a family vacation," replied her dad.

Sure it was, she thought. The idea of spending three entire days and nights sleeping in a tent out in the wilderness that was named after the explorer Daniel Boone did not appeal to her girly side. "Mom, can we stay…?"

Before she could finish, Emily's younger brother came bolting out the door, his suitcase overflowing, and his momentum almost knocking her to the ground. "Let's go, let's go."

Emily climbed into the backseat, her MP3 player blasting loudly; at least she had some piece of civilization left. As they drove for what seemed like forever, Emily enjoyed peering out the window. As they got farther and farther away from the city, she began to catch glimpses of rabbits, squirrels, and various birds that she wasn't used to seeing. The tall buildings and annoying noises of the city began to be replaced by a peaceful quiet. She turned her music off, but kept the ear buds in place, as she didn't want anyone to know that she was enjoying the ride. Finally, she saw the sign: Welcome to the Daniel Boone National Forest.

"Can we hike to the falls?" her brother asked.

She exited the vehicle, declared that she was ready for a walk. She had heard about Cumberland Falls but had never actually seen them. Some of her classmates had mentioned that they were smaller, but a lot like Niagara Falls. She had no desire to let the others know she was excited, but she hoped that her dad would say that they could go exploring.

Looking around her, she saw huge mountains that seemed to tower above the river below. This was much different from the small subdivision that she called home. Just maybe the next three days wouldn't be so bad. As she removed her earbuds, she smiled, as a small deer crossed the pathway several hundred feet in the distance. The first live deer that she had ever seen was when she was twelve. " Wow, this is really amazing! Let's take that walk, Dad."

"Really?" he asked.

Passage 2

Jasmine nervously left the car. She and her parents had been riding for what seemed like days, but after ten hours, they were finally here. She carefully studied the old farmhouse. "Are you ready?" her dad asked. Jasmine only shrugged. She had talked with her "G", as the kind lady had referred to herself, a few times on the phone, but at the age of eight, she had never actually met her grandma. It seemed that work, school, or illness had kept her away.

Jasmine's parents had told her stories about her "G" and that she had met her when she was only a few months old, but in Jasmine's mind this was the first time. She exited the car and was greeted by a petite, black-haired lady, standing in the doorway. Her smile looked familiar. It seemed to be a combination of her own and the warm smile that her dad seldom showed, but that warmed her heart, over and over.

Her "G" had scooped her up. "Come on in here, Jasmine." Jasmine felt a bit nervous, but she walked into the house with her grandmother's arms still around her. I bet you are tired of sitting. "How long have you had my beautiful granddaughter cooped up in that car?" asked her "G". Jasmine's dad replied, "It has been a while."

"Come on, honey. There is so much that I want to show you." her grandma cooed. Jasmine followed her grandmother through the house. It seemed that they exited one doorway, only to enter another. "Here is a surprise for you," her grandma stated. Looking down, Jasmine saw the most beautiful locket. She picked it up, nervously. "I have been saving this for you. It was your great granny's...my mom's." Jasmine pulled it closer for a better view.

"Let me put it on you, you beautiful girl."

4. How are the themes in these passages related?

Ⓐ Both girls have negative feelings about a new situation that they are being made to do. Both of their experiences turned out to be positive.

Ⓑ Both girls have negative feelings about something they are being made to do. Their experiences turn out to be worse than planned.

Ⓒ Both girls are excited to try something new.

Ⓓ Both girls are meeting someone new for the first time.

Question 5 and 6 are based on the passages below

Read BOTH passages, and answer the questions that follow.

Passage 1: Cell Phones in the Classroom

A familiar ringtone sounds in the classroom directing everyone's attention to a shy student in the back row. Several years ago, this would have seemed a bit strange, but not today. A recent study showed that one in three third-grade students have a cell phone. With so many students having access to technology devices, a lot of talks have gone into deciding whether to use them as learning tools or to ban them from the classroom.

Let's think about cell phones' role as learning tools. Annie needs a calculator but forgot hers. She takes out her cell phone and can use the calculator app on the phone. Just across the room, Johnny is trying to spell the word "similar," so he uses the dictionary app on his phone to find the correct spelling. Mitchell, has completed all of his work early, so he decides to use the multiplication app on his phone to review multiplication facts in a fun and interactive way. These devices are causing teachers and other school officials to see that cell phones give students access to resources that actually save schools money.

While cell phones may sound great, not every school district is ready to lift the cell phone ban. There are still those that have major concerns. One concern is what to do about students who do not have a cell phone. Another worry is how to make sure students are using the phone as a learning tool instead of texting and social media. Additional concerns arise with how to address when a phone is broken or stolen while at school. Certainly, the list of problems that some schools have goes on and on.

The answer isn't clear for schools across the United States. Some schools are starting to lift the cell phone ban, but others are keeping it in place. As students pack backpacks with cell phones, the discussion of having them in the classroom will certainly continue.

Passage 2: Always Worked Fine Before

I hear a lot of talk about allowing cell phones in the classroom. Why? There is nothing wrong with the way things are now. If you allow cell phones in classrooms, you are asking for trouble.

Cell phones may distract students to off-task behaviors. Students may tell you that they are playing learning games, but how do you know that they are not sending texts? Students may skip doing their assignments so that they can hurry and play learning games. Cell phones will make classrooms noisier. If everyone gets messages, plays games, or receives phone calls, think about how noisy classrooms will be.

We really do not need cell phones in our classrooms. It seems to me that our classrooms are functioning correctly as they are right now. They are helping prepare me and other students for the future.

5. **According to Passage 1, What is the BIGGEST reason that schools are considering allowing the use of cell phones?**

   Ⓐ Schools are running out of money.
   Ⓑ Cell phones are great educational tools.
   Ⓒ Cell phones could help with the constant stream of school emergencies.
   Ⓓ Parents are forcing schools to allow their kids to have access to their phones.

6. **How are these passages different?**

   Ⓐ One passage is talking about both sides of the cell phone argument. The second passage is talking only about why cell phones are needed in the classroom.
   Ⓑ The first passage is talking about both sides of the cell phone argument. The second passage is talking only about why cell phones are NOT needed in the classroom.
   Ⓒ Both passages are too similar to pick out a difference.
   Ⓓ One passage argues that cell phones cost too much money. The other passage argues that cell phones are too noisy.

The Olympic games have endured for over 100 years. They remain a passion for fans, athletes, and trainers all over the world. While the love of this worldwide event is well-known, many changes have occurred since 1896.

In 1896, the Olympic games had 42 events and 245 competitors. These games were hosted in Athens, Greece. Only 14 nations were represented in the Olympic games. In Greece, A little over one hundred years ago, women were not allowed to participate in the Olympic games. The most successful athlete from the 1896 games was a German wrestler and gymnast named Carl Schumann. Schumann won 4 gold medals.

The 2008 Olympic Games showed how much a century can change things. Over 200 nations were represented in Beijing, China. There were over 10,000 males and females who competed for their chance at gold. A total of over 300 events were completed. The most successful athlete from the 2008 games was American swimmer Michael Phelps. Phelps earned 8 gold medals in the 2008 Olympics. This was a new record for the most gold medals won during a single Olympics event. The 2008 Olympic games marked an end for two popular events: baseball and softball.

While a lot has changed about the Olympic games, some have remained the same. The games are still held every four years. The International Sports Federation Rules continue to apply to the event. The gold, silver, and bronze medals are given today, just as they were 116 years ago in Athens, Greece.

7. Which of the following would be a major change to the present day Olympic games?

    Ⓐ Changing the Olympic Games to be in the same location EVERY year
    Ⓑ Adding new events
    Ⓒ Getting rid of some outdated events
    Ⓓ Adding new countries to those that already participate in the Olympic Games

From McGuffey's Second Eclectic Reader

1.   There are three kinds of bees: workers, drones, and queens.
2.   Bees live in a house that is called a hive.
3.   Only one queen can live in each hive. If she is lost or dead, the other bees will stop their work.
4.   They are very wise and busy little creatures. They all join together to build cells of wax for their honey.
5.   Each bee takes its proper place, and does its own work. Some go out and gather honey from the flowers; others stay at home and work inside the hive.
6.   The cells which they build, are all one shape and size, and there are no spaces between them.
7.   The cells are not round, but have six sides.
8.   Have you ever looked into a glass hive to see the bees at work? They are always busy.

9.	The drones do not work. Every year before winter, all of the drones are driven from the hive or killed. The reason the drones are driven from the hive or killed is because they did not help make the honey.

10.	It is not quite safe for children to handle bees because they have stingers. Bees use their stingers as a great defensive tool.

8. Based on this paragraph, how is the queen bee different from the other bees in the hive?

    Ⓐ	The queen bee is much smaller than the other bees.
    Ⓑ	The queen bee works harder than the other bees.
    Ⓒ	There are more worker bees than there are queen bees.
    Ⓓ	The queen bee lives in the hive while the other bees live outside of the hive.

Question 9 and 10 are based on the story below

Brandon lived with his mother at one end of the forest. His school was at the other end of the forest. Every day he had to go through the forest to get to school and the forest was very scary.

One day he told his mother that he felt very scared to cross that forest.

His mother said, "Don't be scared" "Your brother lives in the forest. Whenever you get scared, you can always call him. He won't answer you but he will see that no harm comes to you."

Brandon said, "Why did you not tell me about my brother earlier? What is his name?"

Mother said, "His name is Courage. Whenever you get frightened, call his name, and he will silently follow you to school and see that you come back home safely."

The next day Brandon was happy to get ready for school. He was not scared as he went through the forest on the way to school. That day, while coming home from school, he got scared when he heard the sounds of animals. He then remembered his mother's words that his brother would protect him whenever he was frightened.

Brandon called out "Courage, Courage" with full confidence. Suddenly he began to feel better. He began to feel brave. He again called out, "Courage!, Courage!" He thought that his brother was silently following him, he began to sing softly and then loudly. He realized that he was not frightened after all. He crossed the forest confidently with courage.

The only thing we need to have is confidence and courage in ourselves to move ahead.

9. How do Brandon's feelings about the forest change from the beginning of the story to the end of the story?

Ⓐ Brandon is scared of the forest at the beginning of the story but because he finds courage he is not scared of the forest at the end of the story.

Ⓑ Brandon's feelings about the forest are the same in the beginning and end of the story.

Ⓒ Brandon loves the forest in the beginning of the story but becomes afraid of the forest at the end of the story.

Ⓓ Brandon actually lives in the city and only dreams of the forest.

10. How does Brandon change as the story moves along?

Ⓐ Brandon becomes less brave.

Ⓑ Brandon becomes more afraid.

Ⓒ Brandon becomes less afraid.

Ⓓ Brandon becomes more and more lost in the forest.

Question 11 and 12 are based on the passage below

The New Year Celebrations in Different Countries

In the United States, the New Year begins every January 1st. On the night before, most people celebrate the coming of the New Year right before and when the clock strikes 12:00 am. People generally make what is called "New Year's Resolutions". In doing so, they choose something that they want to change or make better in their lives. Some may decide to lose weight, save money, get along better with others, or even to quit a bad habit. The resolution is supposed to be kept and followed all during the year. It is a kind of promise a person makes to themselves. People tend to break self-made promises early on in the year.

Chinese New Year

The Chinese New Year, commonly called the Spring Festival in China is celebrated at the changing of the traditional lunisolar calendar"-Chinese calendar. The Chinese celebrate beginning on the first new moon, between what we in the United States know as January 21 and February 20. The Chinese start their celebrations on the evening before and continue to celebrate through until around the 15th day of their first calendar month. The Chinese New Year is centuries old and began as a time to honor ancestors and people of high ranking political and religious statuses. Many of the customs of Chinese New Year continue to be followed not only in China, other Chinese influenced countries, but in the United States, as well. These include the annual family dinner, the complete house cleaning to ward off evil and welcome good, and the many parades, brightly decorated costumes, and wall hangings.

The Indian New Year

Ugadi is the official name given to the festival celebrated as the New Year in India. The name,

Ugadi, means the beginning of a new age. It is celebrated on the first day of the Hindu month, Chaitra, thus marking the beginning of spring. It is thought that the Lord Brahma began creation on this day according to Hindu culture. The celebration is highlighted by the serving of magnificent meals. The festival is also known for the cleaning of houses, and wearing of new clothes. In the Indian calendar, each year has a name. There are 60 names and the names are repeated every 60 years.

11. What ways are the celebrations in China and India similar to one another? Circle the correct answer choice

Ⓐ The celebrations occur at different times and have no similarities.
Ⓑ In both China and India, houses are cleaned and expansive meals are served.
Ⓒ The calendars seem to be similar to one another.
Ⓓ None of the above.

12. Which fact stands out to be unique regarding one of the celebrations and historical information given? Circle the correct answer choice.

Ⓐ China has been celebrating for centuries.
Ⓑ The United States starts celebrating the night before the New Year.
Ⓒ The fact that in India they have 60 different names for each New Year and it repeats itself after 60 years.
Ⓓ China and India celebrate at different times of the year.

Question 13 is based on the passage below

Thomas Jefferson (Founding Father) and Benjamin Franklin (Politician)

Thomas Jefferson, Founding Father and Third President of the United States of America. Apr 13, 1743 - Jul 04, 1826

Thomas Jefferson is known as one of the Founding Fathers of the United States. He helped the Americans to realize they needed to separate from Great Britain (England) and form a new nation. He was the main author of the Declaration of Independence. Before becoming President of the United States in 1800, he was the Vice President under John Adams.

He was born and educated in Virginia. After graduating from college, he became a lawyer. He helped to increase the new United States shipping trade as President. He also organized the Louisiana Purchase which gave the United States more land as its own. He served two terms as President and is considered one of the greatest Presidents of the United States.

Benjamin Franklin- Politician, Author and Inventor Jan 17, 1706 - Apr 17, 1790

Benjamin Franklin was also considered one of the Founding Fathers of the United States of America. He was a well-known author. Many of his writings caused great uproar when the colonies were having such political differences with England (Great Britain). In fact, some people said he was a revolutionary because his literary works helped the people in fighting to leave (separate from) England and become their own country. He is noted for his many inventions, as well. His major inventions were that of electricity, the lightning rod, and a cooking stove. Benjamin Franklin was a former speaker of the Pennsylvania House of Representatives.

His writings include Poor Richard's Almanack. He was focused on improving one's one behavior and even wrote a list of virtues that he tried to improve on throughout his life. He wrote these at the early age of 20.

They are as follows: 1. Temperance, 2. Silence, 3. Order, 4. Resolution, 5. Frugality, 6. Industry, 7. Sincerity, 8. Justice, 9. Moderation, 10. Cleanliness, 11. Tranquility, and 12. Humility. Franklin was an excellent reader, but did not graduate from any well- known school or college. He was as some would say, self- educated. His family did not have the money to send him to school.

13. Now reread both passages, look at the Venn diagram and match the characteristics that are only for "Jefferson", "Franklin" under the respective space provided and the common characters of both under the "Like" space.

Use these detailed characteristics to complete your diagram.

1. Founding Father
2. President of the United States
3. Inventor of electricity, lightning rod, cooking stove
4. Politician
5. Author
6. Lived in the 1700s
7. Helped the colonists in breaking away from England
8. Well remembered in US History
9. Attended college
10. Unable to attend college, but well educated
11. Known to have helped the US acquire the Louisiana Purchase
12. Wrote Poor Richard's Almanack.

Jefferson   Like   Franklin

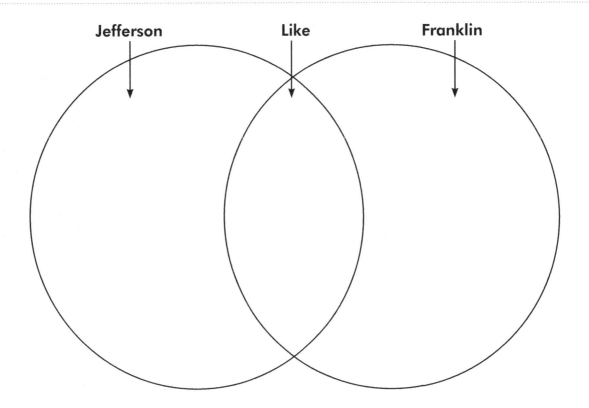

CHAPTER 1 → Lesson 11: Setting the Scene

Question 1-4 are based on the story below

Brandon lived with his mother at one end of the forest. His school was at the other end of the forest. Every day he had to go through the forest to get to school and the forest was very scary.

One day he told his mother that he felt very scared to cross that forest.

His mother said, "Don't be scared" "Your brother lives in the forest. Whenever you get scared, you can always call him. He won't answer you but he will see that no harm comes to you."

Brandon said, "Why did you not tell me about my brother earlier? What is his name?"

Mother said, "His name is Courage. Whenever you get frightened, call his name, and he will silently follow you to school and see that you come back home safely."

The next day Brandon was happy to get ready for school. He was not scared as he went through the forest on the way to school. That day, while coming home from school, he got scared when he heard the sounds of animals. He then remembered his mother's words that his brother would protect him whenever he was frightened.

Brandon called out "Courage, Courage" with full confidence. Suddenly he began to feel better. He began to feel brave. He again called out, "Courage!, Courage!" He thought that his brother was silently following him, he began to sing softly and then loudly. He realized that he was not frightened after all. He crossed the forest confidently with courage.

The only thing we need to have is confidence and courage in ourselves to move ahead.

1. Where did Brandon live?

[ ]

2. In what setting does Brandon find his courage?

- Ⓐ the forest
- Ⓑ his house
- Ⓒ school
- Ⓓ his friend's house

3. Which is a likely setting for this story?

(A) a jungle
(B) a zoo
(C) a forest
(D) on an African safari

4. What does the setting in a story mean? Circle the correct answer choice.

(A) the main person in the story
(B) the time and place where the story happens
(C) the message in the story
(D) the end of the story

Question 5 is based on the story below

An astronomer used to go out every night to observe stars. Often, he would be seen with a telescope in one hand and a notebook in the other. One evening, while he wandered through the suburbs with his attention fixed on the sky, he accidentally fell into a deep uncovered well. He cried out loudly for help. As he waited to be rescued, he moaned and howled about his sores and bruises. His neighbor was passing by and happened to hear his wailing and weeping. He quickly helped him out of the well. After he came to know how the accident happened, this is what he said to the astronomer: "Hark you old fellow, why in striving to pry into heaven, do you not manage to see what is on earth?"

5. Part A

Where does this paragraph take place?

(A) in the astronomer's home
(B) in a planetarium
(C) outdoors at night
(D) outdoors during the day

Part B

How might this story be different if it was set during the day?

(A) The astronomer's neighbor would be able to hear him better during the day.
(B) The astronomer would not have been looking at the stars in the sky, and would have been paying attention to where he was going.
(C) The astronomer would be able to see the stars more clearly during the day.
(D) The astronomer would have been asleep during the day.

Camels are bumpy,
Their backs are all lumpy,
Giraffes are long- legged and meek:
Bears are so growl,
Hyenas are howly,
Dolphins are slippery and sleek.

Kangaroos have a pocket,
But no way to lock it,
Their babies can look out and peep,
But monkeys are funny
I wish I had money,
Enough to buy one and keep.

6. Where does this poem most likely take place?

    Ⓐ   at an amusement park
    Ⓑ   at a veterinarian's office
    Ⓒ   at the zoo
    Ⓓ   in the forest

My First Trip to the Beach

About three weeks ago, Jeremiah's parents surprised him with some news. They were taking him to the beach. He was excited and couldn't wait to tell all of his friends at school.

Soon enough, Friday afternoon arrived. Jeremiah, his sister, his parents, and his nanny all loaded into the car, and set out for the long drive to Destin, Florida. Listening to DVD's grew old rather quickly. A nap was sure to allow Jeremiah to get closer to Florida without growing bored from the ride.

When he awoke from his nap, it was time to stop for dinner. He exited the car, excited to stretch his legs. "Come on, Jeremiah," exclaimed his nanny. He was glad that she had been able to come to the beach. This was also going to be her first time seeing the ocean.

After a quick meal at a fast-food restaurant, the family piled back into the car.

The family arrived at their condo, almost too tired to enjoy the peaceful sound of the ocean. As Jeremiah headed to bed, he knew that the beach would be his to explore in a few hours. He stretched out his small frame across the twin-sized bed and soon fell asleep. He awoke a few hours later, hearing his dad outside on the balcony.

When Jeremiah finally saw the view in the daylight, he was in awe. Beautiful green waters lay off in the distance. They seemed to go on and on, as far as his eyes could see. The sand reminded him of snow.

"Wanna go for a walk?" asked his dad.

Jeremiah smiled, "Yes!" Running back inside, he threw his shoes on. His dad said that he didn't want to try to wear those in the soft, grainy sand. He dressed, and then off they went.

"What's this?" asked Jeremiah, pointing to a loose mound of sand.
"This is a sand dune, it keeps the buildings safe," his dad replied.

"Oh, okay…" Jeremiah and his dad walked along the ocean's edge. There were few words spoken, but the looks on their faces expressed feelings of happiness, as they walked along the beautiful water's edge.

7. Which of the following BEST describes the family's vacation destination?

- Ⓐ the beach
- Ⓑ Destin, Florida
- Ⓒ across state lines
- Ⓓ somewhere with a lot of water

Question 8 is based on the passage below

Directions: Read the following play. Then answer the question that follows.
BROCK: (Brock enters the stage.) What a great day it is.
TERRY: (Snarls) What's good about it?
BROCK: (Laughs) I found something outside on the playground.
TERRY: (Rolls eyes).
MRS. ADAMS: (Walks over). Good morning, boys.
BROCK AND TERRY: Good morning.
MRS. ADAMS: (MOTIONS). Sit down, boys.
TERRY: (Pushes Brock.)
BROCK: Why did you do that? (In a rather loud voice).
TERRY: (Throws hands into the air and pushes Brock again).
MRS. ADAMS: (Runs over). Boys, is this how we want to start the week off?
TERRY: (Sighs.) But, Brock says it is a great day, and…
MRS. ADAMS: (Looks confused). You are upset, just because Brock is happy?
TERRY: (Shakes head no).
BROCK: I don't know what's wrong with him.
TERRY: (Reaches into his pocket.) My mom gave me twenty dollars to pay for my lunch bill, but I can't find it. She is going to be really mad.
BROCK: (Smiles)

MRS. ADAMS: When did you last have the money?
BROCK: (Reaches into his pocket.) Remember that I told you I found something?
TERRY: (Nods).
BROCK: (Hands money to Terry). I found this outside. I bet you dropped it.
TERRY: (Hugs Brock).

8. Where is the setting for this play?

- (A) inside of a classroom
- (B) outside on the playground
- (C) at Terry's house
- (D) at the park

Question 9 is based on the story below

Jasmine nervously left the car. She and her parents had been riding for what seemed like days, but after ten hours, they were finally here. She carefully studied the old farmhouse. "Are you ready?" her dad asked. Jasmine only shrugged. She had talked with her "G", as the kind lady had referred to herself, a few times on the phone, but at the age of eight, she had never actually met her grandma. It seemed that work, school, or illness had kept her away.

Jasmine's parents had told her stories about her "G" and that she had met her when she was only a few months old, but in Jasmine's mind this was the first time. She exited the car and was greeted by a petite, black-haired lady, standing in the doorway. Her smile looked familiar. It seemed to be a combination of her own and the warm smile that her dad seldom showed, but that warmed her heart, over and over.

Her "G" had scooped her up. "Come on in here, Jasmine." Jasmine felt a bit nervous, but she walked into the house with her grandmother's arms still around her. I bet you are tired of sitting. "How long have you had my beautiful granddaughter cooped up in that car?" asked her "G".

Jasmine's dad replied, "It has been a while."

"Come on, honey. There is so much that I want to show you." her grandma cooed. Jasmine followed her grandmother through the house. It seemed that they exited one doorway, only to enter another. "Here is a surprise for you," her grandma stated. Looking down, Jasmine saw the most beautiful locket. She picked it up, nervously. "I have been saving this for you. It was your great granny's...my mom's." Jasmine pulled it closer for a better view.

"Let me put it on you, you beautiful girl."

9. Which of the following BEST describes Jasmine's location in this story?

    Ⓐ At her home
    Ⓑ At her daddy's house
    Ⓒ At her friend's house
    Ⓓ At her G's house

End of Reading Literature

Chapter 2 - Reading Informational Text

Lesson 1: Explicitly Comprehension

Question 1-3 are based on the passage below

The Blues

The Blues is a genre of music that can be directly traced to the "Deep South". The Blues were influenced by a mixture of traditional African music and Southern spirituals. The bedrock of the Blues is set in the Mississippi Delta, where many of the most influential Blues musicians were born. Many of these musicians are self-taught artists. This genre of music has influenced other music genres such as Rock and Roll, Rap, and Country.

One of the most famous Mississippi Delta Blues artists was a man named Robert Johnson. His ability to play the guitar has spawned numerous stories of his ability to play the guitar so well. No matter what story you choose to believe, it is undeniable that Mr. Johnson inspired many future artists with his unique playing style. So the next time you hear your favorite song, ask yourself if you believe that the Blues had some influence on that song.

1. According to the passage where was Robert Johnson from?

Ⓐ The passage does not state specifically where Robert Johnson was from.
Ⓑ Robert Johnson was from Chicago.
Ⓒ The passage states that Robert Johnson was from the Mississippi Delta.
Ⓓ Robert Johnson was from Africa.

2. Where did the Blues begin?

Ⓐ The Blues began in Africa.
Ⓑ The passage states that the Blues began in the Deep South.
Ⓒ The Blues began in Europe according to the passage.
Ⓓ The Blues began in the Northern states of the U.S.

3. What type of music does the passage say that the Blues has influenced?

Ⓐ The passage does not say that the blues have influenced any other type of music.
Ⓑ The passage states that the Blues have influenced Rock and Roll, Rap, and Country.
Ⓒ The passage says that the Blues have only influenced classical music.
Ⓓ The passage says that the Blues have only influenced guitar players.

THE WATER CYCLE

The water cycle is a cycle that repeats itself over and over again. After it rains, you may see a lot of water puddles on the ground. Then the sun comes out and the puddles disappear. Did you know the sun will then change the water on the ground into a gas called "water vapor"? This part of the water cycle is called evaporation (liquid changed to a gas). As the water vapor rises into the air, it sticks with pieces of dust. The air gets cooler and the vapor changes back into liquid (water). This is called condensation. The condensation collects and forms clouds. When there is too much water for the clouds to hold, the cloud bursts and precipitation falls back to earth as rain, snow, sleet, or hail. This cycle continues again and again. Evaporation, condensation, and precipitation are the processes involved in the water cycle.

4. According to the passage what does evaporation mean?

- Ⓐ   The air gets cooler and the vapor changes back to liquid.
- Ⓑ   The liquid changes to a gas.
- Ⓒ   The condensation collects and forms clouds.
- Ⓓ   The gas changes to liquid.

Good manners can be seen at home, at school, on the playground, and at the dining table where we eat our meals. A well-mannered person is polite and gentle when he talks.
Everyone likes a person who is polite and well-mannered. Good manners are always liked by everyone and bring good rewards.

All that is right pleases everyone. Therefore, we should do what is right always. We should always remember to do what is right.

All that is wrong displeases everyone. Therefore, we should not do what is wrong. We will be rewarded for our good actions.

A boy or girl who constantly comes late for work cannot be depended upon. People do not give him or her any important work for they do not know whether he/she will come on time or not. A person who is always late loses friends.

All of us make mistakes. When we make a mistake, we do not like to be punished for it. We like to be forgiven. Therefore, we too should forgive the mistakes of others. Forgiveness is a great virtue.

It is easy to make a mistake, but it is not easy to forget that mistake. If we make some mistake, we should feel sorry for it. We should also apologize to the person whom we have hurt.

We should not cheat on an examination. Cheating always does more harm than good. We should not keep bad company.

5. What title best shows what this selection is MOSTLY about?

Ⓐ Good Virtues
Ⓑ Stealing
Ⓒ Late Coming
Ⓓ Examinations

6. Why does everyone like a person who is good-mannered?

Ⓐ Because he answers rudely.
Ⓑ Because he talks out of turn.
Ⓒ Because he is polite and gentle.
Ⓓ Because he shouts at everyone.

7. According to this selection, what pleases others?

Ⓐ Doing what is right.
Ⓑ Telling lies.
Ⓒ Being stubborn.
Ⓓ Talking ill of others.

8. Why is 'late coming' a bad habit?

Ⓐ Because late comers will not do any work.
Ⓑ Because it is good to come late.
Ⓒ Because late comers cannot be depended upon.
Ⓓ Because late comers go late.

9. According to the selection, do we like anyone to punish us for our mistakes? Why?

Ⓐ No, we like to be forgiven.
Ⓑ We like to get punished.
Ⓒ We never get punished.
Ⓓ We do not like to be forgiven.

Pearl reached in her pocket for the coins, but she could not feel them. Desperately, she pulled everything out of her pocket. She found a chocolate wrapper, a bus pass, her student ID card, lipstick, mascara, and her cell phone. There were no coins!

10. Which items in Pearl's pocket shows the reader she is a teenager, not a young child?

Ⓐ The makeup
Ⓑ The bus pass
Ⓒ The student ID
Ⓓ All of the above

States in the US

Look at the map. Then read the list of states in ABC order. Note that the states of Hawaii and Alaska are not shown in the correct location. The reason for this is simple. Alaska is located on the end of Canada far above Washington to the left. One side of Alaska is located on the Pacific Ocean. It is not connected to the rest of the US. The state of Hawaii is a group of islands located in the Pacific Ocean and again is not adjoined to the US. Thus it, too, would not fit correctly on this map. The Pacific Ocean is on the left of the map in blue, the Gulf of Mexico is on the bottom in blue and flows into the Atlantic Ocean on the right in blue.

Carefully review all that you read, and see before answering the questions below.

The Fifty States in ABC Order:

Alabama, Alaska, Arizona, Arkansas, California,
Colorado, Connecticut
Delaware, Florida, Georgia, Hawaii, Idaho, Illinois,
Indiana
Iowa, Kansas, Kentucky, Louisiana, Maine,
Maryland, Massachusetts, Michigan.
Minnesota, Mississippi, Missouri, Montana,
Nebraska, Nevada,
New Hampshire, New Jersey, New Mexico, New York,
North Carolina, North Dakota, Ohio,
Oklahoma, Oregon, Pennsylvania, Rhode Island,
South Carolina,
South Dakota, Tennessee, Texas,
Utah, Vermont, Virginia, Washington, West Virginia,
Wisconsin, Wyoming.

After reviewing the facts given, the map and the list of states in ABC order, answer the questions.

11. Where is Hawaii located?

12. Where is Alaska located?

13. How many states begin with the letter T?

14. Which letters in the alphabet are not used for state names? List them.

Question 15 is based on the passage below

Playing Video Games

Scotty loves to play video games! I mean he plays every chance he gets. He even plays when he should be doing his homework, chores or going to bed! It has gotten so bad that his parents are considering a punishment to teach him a lesson.

Scotty doesn't understand why they are upset with him and is trying to figure out what he can do so that he doesn't get his video game machine taken away. He has asked his friends for their ideas on the subject, too. He even asked his counselor at school. Scotty has been seeing her since his grades started dropping. The counselor told him it is very simple, give up the game playing on his own and get back to doing homework, chores, and going to bed on time.

To Scotty, the ideas his counselor told him are good, but he is very reluctant to do it. So one of his friends, Hailey, has offered to help. She is going to make him a chart of time spent on playing games compared to time spent on his responsibilities. He agrees to give it a try.

15. Who should Scotty share his chart with? Circle the correct answer choice.

Ⓐ His counselor
Ⓑ His parents
Ⓒ His friend, Hailey
Ⓓ All of the above

CHAPTER 2 → Lesson 2: The Main Idea Arena

Question 1 and 2 are based on the passage below

After reading the passage, enter the details in the map below. This will help you to answer the questions that follow.

Everything in nature follows a pattern. Circles, lines, spirals, and angles are repeated to make a design or a pattern. Patterns in nature are not just pretty adornments. They serve a purpose that has helped nature survive and flourish.

Have you ever taken a close look at a beehive? Well, not too close or you might get stung! The natural pattern in beehives is so perfect that it seems to be computer designed. The hives are made up of layers and layers of cells. Each cell has six perfectly equal sides or hexagons. Why would bees build six-sided cells, instead of round, or box shaped ones? The reason is that the bee is a genius at geometry and architecture! Six-sided cells use up every bit of space and allow bees to get the maximum area for storing honey. Also, hexagons use the least honeycomb wax because all six sides are identical in length. The bees don't waste space, material, or effort. Aren't they smart insects?

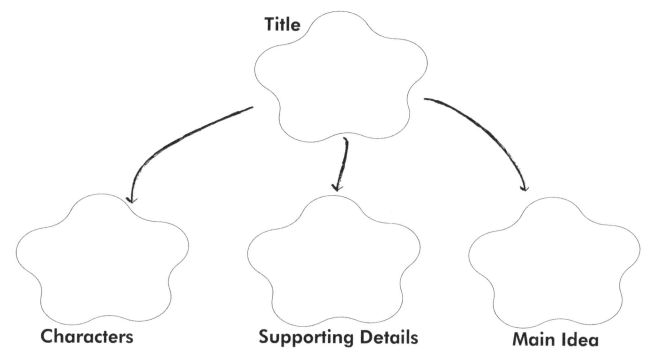

Title

Characters   **Supporting Details**   **Main Idea**

1. What is the main idea of the selection?

Ⓐ   Beehives have a disorganized pattern.
Ⓑ   Every cell in the beehive has a different shape.
Ⓒ   Every cell in the beehive has five sides.
Ⓓ   Everything in nature follows a pattern.

2. What is the above passage telling us?

Ⓐ It's introducing the reader to patterns.
Ⓑ It tells us how bees makes use of patterns.
Ⓒ It tells us how patterns are used only by people.
Ⓓ It tells us how bees have limited intelligence.

Question 3 and 4 are based on the passage below

After reading the passage, enter the details in the map below. This will help you to answer the questions that follow.

A robot is a device that can do tasks that are difficult or impossible for human beings. A robot does not have to be shaped like a person; robots can be shaped like animals or machines. Law enforcement agencies have robots that can go into dangerous areas, which might cause injury to individuals and thereby help in maintaining law and order with ease. Medical facilities have microscopic robot cameras that go into areas of the human body, robot cameras bloodstreams, that are too small for a doctor to see. Military units have robotic devices such as drone airplanes that can deliver bombs without risk to the soldiers who are operating the planes. Robots are also being sent into outer space to explore areas that are too dangerous for humans to visit.

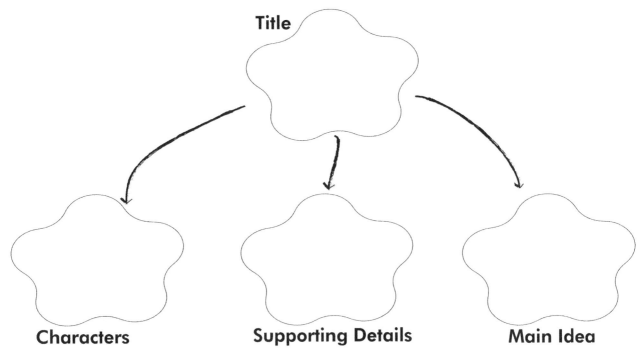

Title

Characters   **Supporting Details**   **Main Idea**

3. What is the main idea in this passage?

Ⓐ Robots can be shaped like animals or machines.
Ⓑ A robot is a device that can do tasks that would be difficult or impossible for human beings.
Ⓒ Law enforcement, agencies have robots that can go into dangerous areas where a person could be injured.
Ⓓ A robot does not have to be shaped like a person.

4. Which sentence in the passage gives a detail that does not support the main idea?

Ⓐ A robot does not have to be shaped like a person; robots can be shaped like animals or machines.

Ⓑ Military units use robotic devices such as drone airplanes that can deliver bombs without risk to the soldiers who are operating the planes.

Ⓒ Robots are being sent into outer space to explore areas that would be dangerous for humans to visit.

Ⓓ Law enforcement, agencies have robots that can go into dangerous areas where a person might be injured.

5. Which sentence in the paragraph is its main idea?

1. The thermometer read -15. 2. The edges of Jeremy's ears were stinging with cold. 3. He wished he had put on two pairs of socks. 4. His forehead was numb. 5. He couldn't feel his fingers any longer. 6. This was the coldest day he had ever lived through.

Ⓐ Sentence 2.
Ⓑ Sentence 5.
Ⓒ Sentence 6.
Ⓓ Sentence 1.

6. Which sentence in the paragraph shows its main idea?

1. All of Jennifer's favorites were on the table. 2. There was corn on the cob. 3. There were mashed potatoes with gravy, and fried chicken. 4. There was frosty lemonade to drink. 5. There were straw-berries with whipped cream for dessert.

Ⓐ Sentence 1.
Ⓑ Sentence 2.
Ⓒ Sentence 4.
Ⓓ Sentence 5.

7. Which sentence in the paragraph shows its main idea?

1. Joe was as surprised as anyone when he won the race. 2. He hadn't done nearly enough condi-tioning. 3. He hadn't eaten a good breakfast that morning. 4. He hadn't gotten enough sleep last night 5. The other runners were very fast. 6. In spite of all those problems, Joe was the fastest guy on the track and he left all the other runners behind.

Ⓐ Sentence 4.
Ⓑ Sentence 2.
Ⓒ Sentence 5.
Ⓓ Sentence 6.

8. Which sentence in the paragraph shows its main idea?

1. The gifts were wonderful. 2. The guests were courteous and cheerful. 3. The food was delicious. 4. The decorations were beautiful. 5. It was a perfect party in every way.

    Ⓐ Sentence 1.
    Ⓑ Sentence 3.
    Ⓒ Sentence 2.
    Ⓓ Sentence 5.

9. Which sentence in the paragraph shows its main idea?

1. Karen had never had such a miserable day. 2. She was seasick as the tiny tourist boat pulled out to sea. 3. She wished she had waited back on shore. 4. It was cold on the boat and she hadn't brought a jacket. 5. She didn't know any of the other passengers, and no one seemed to want to talk to her.

    Ⓐ Sentence 1.
    Ⓑ Sentence 2.
    Ⓒ Sentence 3.
    Ⓓ Sentence 5.

10. What sentence is the main idea of this paragraph?

1. For one thing, he never answered the phone when the citizens called to ask him questions. 2. For another thing, he was rude to them when they tried to get his attention. 3. For another thing, he was getting richer every day, as the townspeople became poorer. 4. In short, he was the worst mayor the little town had ever seen.

    Ⓐ Sentence 1
    Ⓑ Sentence 2
    Ⓒ Sentence 3
    Ⓓ Sentence 4

Question 11 is based on the passage below

What do you see?

Have you ever laid down on your back in a green field on a bright sunny day and gazed up at the clouds? I do it all the time when I get a chance. It can be so much fun to see what you can see in a fluffy cloud or groups of clouds. Look at one that has a thin long end, several little ends coming down in the middle and a much bigger other end...What do you see? It might be a dog. Yes, look, there are the ears on top! It could even be a lion with the larger end opening up like its mouth.

Then start to find many clouds. How many different animals or plants or even people can you locate?

See how they are similar or different in both size and formation.

Try doing this with a group of friends and the possibilities are endless. This kind of activity can help to stimulate your brain better than any video game or TV show! Take a sketch pad or drawing tablet with you. You will be surprised at how easy it can be to draw these! Have one of your buddies close their eyes. Describe the cloud you are looking at. Next have your friend open up their eyes and find the cloud in the sky that you described. Keep a record of who can tell which cloud was the right one. But, be careful, clouds can change their formations sometimes rather quickly!

Before answering the questions, try rereading the passage to get a better understanding of the author's message.

Hint: The author is describing an event and things that you might try to do.

11. Which sentence best summarizes the above selection? Select the right answer choice by circling it.

 Ⓐ Clouds are everywhere.
 Ⓑ Watching clouds is better than playing video games.
 Ⓒ Watching clouds by yourself or with friends can be enjoyable, fun and can stimulate your brain.
 Ⓓ You can describe clouds to other people.

Question 12 is based on the passage below

Who says guys only cook on the grill

My grandma, mom and sister always do the cooking in the kitchen at our house. It is very good indeed, do not get me wrong. Sometimes, however, I would like to cook on the stove, too! Dad says that guys do the grilling on the bbq pit outside. Why can't we cook inside, too?

So one day I asked Dad, "Dad, what would you like for supper tonight?" He replied, "Gee, Howard, I would really love hamburger steak with onions, but your mom doesn't want to cook that."

I announced, "Please, let me try to cook it!" Mom and Dad looked at each other and nodded yes.

I was so elated! First thing I did was ask Mom if she had everything we needed. She said she had no idea what we needed. So I looked on our computer under recipes and found several. I began to read off the ingredients. Some she had already and some she said we do not use. I decided to combine a couple of recipes and make my own. Here it is!

Ingredients for the hamburger steak patties:

1 to 1 ½ lbs of hamburger meat- preferably the ground chuck

3-4 tablespoons of cooking oil, we use canola

1 large egg

2/3 cups of really fine chopped onions

1 teaspoon of Worchester sauce- spicy sauce if you would rather

A pinch of salt

A pinch of garlic powder

A pinch of black pepper
About 1/3-1/2 cup of all-purpose flour- use that to coat the patties to brown

Now, the gravy:

Instead of making homemade gravy, Dad and I decided I could use the package of onion gravy mix- I used 2 packages!

A half of an onion sliced real thin, long slices!

A little more Worchester sauce for flavor- a splash or two

Directions:

Take the ingredients for the hamburger steak patties and mix them together- do not add the flour. Form large patties, it will probably make at least 5-6. Flatten as much as you can, but not too thin. Now pat the flour on each side of the patties. In a very large frying pan or skillet, heat your cooking oil until it starts to bubble just a bit. Now place the patties in the oil and cook on each side for about 4-5 minutes until brown. Remove them from the frying pan. Lay aside, but keep warm. (Warning, do not try to flatten your patties, as it will cause them to fall apart. One of mine did fall apart.)

While the pan is still hot and on, add the thinly sliced onions. Let them cook until they start to turn a little brown. Now, lower the flame and add the gravy mix according to the package. Turn the flame back up and let it come to a low boil. Be sure to use a spoon or ladle and stir the gravy while it is cooking.

Let the gravy mix cook on low for about 5 minutes. Add more water a little at a time if it thickens too fast. Now take the patties and add them to the gravy mix. Cover with a lid and cook for no more than 20 minutes on low.

Enjoy! We did! Yes, now my grandma, mom and sister let me cook inside any time I want to try a new recipe! Who says guys only cook on the grill?

12. Read the steps given below. Arrange it in the correct sequence of the recipe.

    A. Remove the patties and set aside but keep them warm.
    B. Mix the hamburger steak patty ingredients without the flour and make patties.
    C. Cook the patties in the onion and onion gravy mix for about 20 minutes.
    D. Now add the onion gravy mix according to the package directions.
    E. Cover patties with flour and cook about 5 minutes until brown on each side.
    F. Take the thinly sliced onions, add them to the pan and cook a little.

Question 13 is based on the passage below

Monarch Butterflies- The King of Butterflies

The Monarch butterfly travels very far each fall. Millions of monarch butterflies leave the Great Lakes and New York areas and fly to Mexico. It takes what is called the fourth generation cycle for this to happen. This means that the first three generations do not make it to Mexico. Some scientists believe they do this to get away from the cold weather. Mexico has reserved and dedicated mountain regions as preserved lands for the species. The butterflies stay in Mexico until the next summer. Then they travel back to the Great Lakes and New York area where they lay eggs, and then die. The life cycle of the monarch butterfly that goes to Mexico is about eight to nine months after becoming an adult. Butterflies have what is considered to be four life cycle stages. The female monarch lands on milkweed leaves to begin the process. The mother chooses the milkweed so that the caterpillar can eat off of the leaves. The first stage is eggs being laid, the larvae comes next-caterpillar, and then is the pupa stage- the chrysalis and finally the adult. The caterpillar is grown in around 2 weeks. He then finds a stem to attach itself so it can go through the process of metamorphosis. During this stage of major changes, he stays inside the chrysalis.

Once the monarch emerges it is so beautiful that it is often called the King of Butterflies!

13. How long do adult monarch butterflies usually live once they are adults and travel many miles? Circle the correct option.

Ⓐ They usually live to be about ten months old.
Ⓑ They usually live to be about eight to nine months old.
Ⓒ They die within 10 days after being laid as eggs.
Ⓓ None of the above.

Question 14 is based on the passage below

Fishing Industries Along the Gulf Coast

If you live in the area of the United States known as the Southern Gulf Coast, along the Gulf of Mexico, you live in Texas, Louisiana, Mississippi, Alabama or Florida. The Gulf Coast has been called the Fishing Capital of the United States by many people. From Brownsville to the Florida Keys, fisherman go out into the gulf waters in their boats to make a living off of the fish, shrimp, crab, and other seafood they catch.

Trawler is the name usually given when talking about the shrimp and fish boats that go out into the Gulf of Mexico along the established waters to bring in catches. These boats that go out in the gulf are generally about 70' long or longer and most all are refrigerated and steel hull boats now. The refrigeration helps the boat captain to stay out for extended periods of time, ranging anywhere from

3 to about 14 days. Before refrigeration was common on trawlers, the boats would have to go in to a port to dock and get more ice or come back to their home port frequently. Steel hull trawlers are much sturdier than the old wooden hull boats that could be easily damaged by storms, hitting sunken boats or other objects.

Boats or trawlers have a bunk house (sleeping quarters), galley (kitchen), bathroom, and a wheel-house. The trawlers are equipped with high tech radios and equipment in the wheelhouse to help the crew find areas of fish and shrimp. Thus little time is wasted in putting their nets down and dragging the bottom of the gulf to find the seafood they need to bring in.

The people working on a trawler are most often referred to as the crew. The crew consists of the cap-tain (sometimes the owner, sometimes not- whose job it is to run the boat, steer, and make sure all the crew are working), the deck hands (deck hands help to keep the nets in order, repair as needed while out at sea, dropping nets in the water and hauling them in), headers (people head the shrimp as the nets are hauled in, clean fish, and store the catch.), and usually a separate man, the cook, whose only job is to keep the boat clean, and keep the crew well fed. Although some women do work on the boats, more often than not, the boat crew is all male.

The fishing industry is vital to the economy on the Southern Gulf Coast. It is estimated that in the en-tire US, this industry employs over 1.6 million people. On the Gulf Coast alone, the industry brings in over 22.6 billion dollars to aid the economy.

14. Write a sentence of your own explaining the benefit of refrigeration as related to the fishing industry. Use facts from the passage to help you.

Hobbies are Good for the Mind and Body

Many people enjoy hobbies. They can range from designing arts and crafts to singing in a choir. Hobbies improve self-esteem, physical well-being and can increase your academic gains, as well.

Arts and crafts have been known to enable you to gain higher fine motor skills while creating unique works of art. Learning how to work slowly and taking time to complete projects can help you to learn self- control, and develop patience. Some forms of arts and crafts include drawing, painting, building model cars, model airplanes, jewelry making, and leather work. There are many arts and craft stores where you can find your interests.

Sports have always been great hobbies for the young and old. Team and individual sports include football, baseball, soccer, swimming, tennis, wrestling and more. Quite often you join a sport to be with friends, learn to develop physical strength, or to enjoy what you like doing most. Communities generally have organizations to help parents and their children find the best sport for them.

Another form of hobby includes collecting. You can start collecting sports cards, and comic books at an early age. Doll collections, kept in pristine condition over the years can even be a financial plus when you get older. Your parents and relatives can help you start your collection if you ask them to give you collectible items you want for birthday presents or other occasions.

Did you know that even the performing arts are considered a hobby? Joining a ballet class, drama club, tap and gymnastics, theatre or choir, can be your hobby. Again these types of hobbies help develop physical and emotional skills to improve your health and well-being.

15. **Which is NOT the best way to summarize the selection about hobbies? Circle the correct answer choice.**

   Ⓐ Hobbies help you physically, emotionally, and can improve your life.
   Ⓑ Hobbies can be fun and help you get along with others.
   Ⓒ Hobbies include many things that people like to do.
   Ⓓ Hobbies take a lot of time and can be expensive to do.

CHAPTER 2 → Lesson 3: Cause and Effect

Question 1 is based on the passage below

The Bluegrass State

There is one state with water, wildlife, and mountains. Does this sound too good to be true? Well, it isn't all of these natural features are in The Bluegrass State. Kentucky is home to wonderful lakes that offer fun water activities. These are some of the reasons that people visit Kentucky.

The Bluegrass State has a lot to offer for those looking for fun in the water. Cumberland Falls is a huge waterfall. It has been nicknamed "the Niagara of the South". If you are looking to do more than just see the water, a visit to beautiful Lake Cumberland might be a good stop for you. Here you can enjoy boating, fishing, or jet skiing.

Maybe, you are more of a wildlife person. Many people love hunting in the western part of the state. Natural wildlife can be found throughout the area. There are excursions in the Daniel Boone National Forest that are great also.

If this does not sound like fun to you, then you might like to learn more about Kentucky's horses. You can visit one of the race tracks or horse farms. Visitors from all over the world have visited Churchill Downs. Their horses race in the Kentucky Derby. Several other races that can be attended throughout the year. Other locations that allow you to enjoy Kentucky's best thoroughbreds include the Kentucky Horse Park and Keeneland.

Kentucky's tourism doesn't stop there. Guests can visit Mammoth Cave and the home of Abraham Lincoln. Certainly, the Bluegrass State is filled with features that keep people visiting this beautiful state.

1. **Which of the following probably happened BEFORE tourists started visiting Kentucky to see the exciting race horses?**

   Ⓐ Churchill Downs was built.
   Ⓑ Lake Cumberland was developed.
   Ⓒ The Daniel Boone National Forest was named.
   Ⓓ The owners of Keeneland invited guests from all around the world.

Amelia Earhart

Amelia Earhart was born on July 24, 1897. She lived with her grandparents until the age of 12 when she and her sister went to live with their parents in 1909. Amelia's plans were to attend college, but when she came across four wounded World War I soldiers, she decided that she wanted to become a nurse. Her dedication to helping people led her from nursing to work as a social worker. While she worked as a social worker, she often spent her free time teaching immigrant children how to speak English.

Her most noteworthy journey began in 1920 when she took a ten-minute plane ride that completely changed her life. She decided to focus on earning a pilot's license. She challenged herself with a variety of jobs to earn the $1,000 needed for flying lessons to fulfill her dream.

Amelia Earhart proceeded to excel as a pilot. She received a medal from President Herbert Hoover in 1932 for her solo flight across the Atlantic. She did not stop there. Earhart was the first female to fly from Hawaii to California.

Amelia Earhart's contribution to history ended on July 2, 1937, when a frantic message was received by the U. S. Coast Guard. The message was from Earhart stating that she and the plane were in trouble. The plane went down, and no one has ever seen Earhart again. Her devotion to creating change remains a legacy. This legacy emphasizes how setting dreams and achieving goals can be done through hard work and determination.

2. Which sentence indicates why Earhart never went to college?

Ⓐ She lived with her grandparents until the age of 12 when she and her sister went to live with their parents in 1909.

Ⓑ Amelia's plans were to attend college, but when she came across four wounded World War I soldiers, she decided that she wanted to become a nurse.

Ⓒ Her dedication to helping people led her from nursing to work as a social worker, where she spent her free time teaching immigrant children the English language.

Ⓓ Her most noteworthy journey began in 1920 when she took a ten-minute plane ride that forever changed her life.

Cell Phones in the Classroom

A familiar ringtone sounds in the classroom directing everyone's attention to a shy student in the back row. Several years ago, this would have seemed a bit strange, but not today. A recent study showed that one in three third-grade students have a cell phone. With so many students having access to technology devices, a lot of talks have gone into deciding whether to use them as learning tools or to ban them from the classroom.

Let's think about cell phones' role as learning tools. Annie needs a calculator but forgot hers. She takes out her cell phone and can use the calculator app on the phone. Just across the room, Johnny is trying to spell the word "similar," so he uses the dictionary app on his phone to find the correct spelling. Mitchell, has completed all of his work early, so he decides to use the multiplication app on his phone to review multiplication facts in a fun and interactive way. These devices are causing teachers and other school officials to see that cell phones give students access to resources that actually save schools money.

While cell phones may sound great, not every school district is ready to lift the cell phone ban. There are still those that have major concerns. One concern is what to do about students who do not have a cell phone. Another worry is how to make sure students are using the phone as a learning tool instead of texting and social media. Additional concerns arise with how to address when a phone is broken or stolen while at school. Certainly, the list of problems that some schools have goes on and on.

The answer isn't clear for schools across the United States. Some schools are starting to lift the cell phone ban, but others are keeping it in place. As students pack backpacks with cell phones, the discussion of having them in the classroom will certainly continue.

3. **What does the author state would be a positive effect of allowing students to have cell phones in the classroom?**

   Ⓐ Students could access learning apps to assist in learning.
   Ⓑ Students could stay in touch with their family and friends throughout the school by texting.
   Ⓒ Students could stay connected through social media.
   Ⓓ The school would have to buy students a new phone if their phone was broken or stolen while at school.

Question 4-6 are based on the passage below

THE WATER CYCLE

The water cycle is a cycle that repeats itself over and over again. After it rains, you may see lots of water puddles on the ground. Then the sun comes out and the puddles disappear. Did you know the sun will then change the water on the ground into a gas called "water vapor"? This part of the water cycle is called evaporation (liquid changed to a gas). As the water vapor rises into the air, it sticks with pieces of dust. The air gets cooler and the vapor changes back into liquid (water). This is called condensation. The condensation collects and forms clouds. When there is too much water for the clouds to hold, precipitation falls back to earth as rain, snow, sleet, or hail. This cycle continues again and again. Evaporation, condensation, and precipitation are the processes involved in the water cycle.

4. **What stage in the water cycle is complete when the water falls back to the ground?**

   Ⓐ precipitation
   Ⓑ condensation
   Ⓒ evaporation
   Ⓓ perspiration

5. **Choose the sentence that BEST explains what happens during evaporation.**

   Ⓐ The hot sun beats down on the earth and changes the water to water vapor.
   Ⓑ The water is turned into liquid.
   Ⓒ The water is formed into sleet, rain, snow, or hail.
   Ⓓ Water does not evaporate.

6. **Which of the following activities shows the results of condensation?**

   Ⓐ The rain begins to beat heavily on the roof.
   Ⓑ Jimmy's birthday party is at 1:00. He keeps looking at the sky, watching it become filled with black, dark clouds.
   Ⓒ The hot sun makes playing outside very hard.
   Ⓓ The snow falls, turning everything into a perfect white blanket.

Over the past 100 years, the Olympic games have endured. They remain a passion for fans, athletes, and trainers all over the world. While the love for this worldwide event is well-known, many changes have occurred since 1896.

In 1896, the Olympic games had 42 events and 245 competitors. These games were hosted in Athens, Greece. Only 14 nations were represented in those Olympic games. While only a little over one hundred years ago, women were not allowed to participate in the Olympic games. The most successful athlete from the 1896 games was a German wrestler/gymnast named Carl Schumann. Schumann won 4 gold medals.

The 2008 Olympic Games showed just how much a century can change things. Over 200 nations were represented in Beijing, China. There were over 10,000 males and females who competed for their chance at gold. A total of over 300 events were completed. Meanwhile, the most successful athlete from the 2008 games was American swimmer Michael Phelps. Phelps earned 8 gold medals in the 2008 Olympics. This was a new record for the most gold medals won during a single Olympic game. The 2008 Olympic games also marked an end for two popular events: baseball and softball. While a lot has changed about the Olympic games, some things remain the same. The games are still held every four years. Additionally, the International Sports Federation Rules apply to the event. There are gold, silver, and bronze medals given today, just as they were 116 years ago in Athens, Greece.

7. **Which of the following events MOST LIKELY contributed to the grand success of the Olympics as it is today?**

   Ⓐ The original Olympics were held in Greece the 1800s.
   Ⓑ The 2008 Olympic games
   Ⓒ Phelps victorious performance in 2008, earning him 8 gold medals.
   Ⓓ The first American-hosted Olympic games in 1904.

The Asteroid Belt

It's shaped like a doughnut, made from lumps of rock, and looks like a pattern of floating rocks moving in a circle. This strange sounding object is the Asteroid Belt. The Asteroid Belt was formed from lumps of rock left over after other planets formed. Yes, it is shaped like a doughnut and can be found between the orbits of Mars and Jupiter. The Asteroid Belt has two layers. The inner layer has asteroids made of metals. The outer layer has rocky asteroids.

When you look at the Asteroid Belt it looks like floating rocks moving in a circle. Scientists say that there are millions of asteroids in this belt. It may sound pretty funny, but scientists say that there is still a lot of empty space. As you have probably already guessed, the Asteroid Belt is pretty big. It is actually 215 million miles wide. Jupiter keeps the asteroids inside the belt and prevents them from hitting the planets in space. Jupiter's gravity is what holds the asteroids in place.

The chunks of rock inside of the belt were named asteroid, meaning star and rock. The first asteroids seen in the belt were named after gods and heroes. The first largest asteroid found was named Ceres after a Roman goddess. Ceres was discovered on January 1, 1801. It is the size of Texas, and is it called a dwarf planet. Before an asteroid is named, a group of people check to make sure it is not an inappropriate name. Now that most Roman hero names have been used up, scientists are using the name of the astrophysicist to name an asteroid. A lot of information remains unknown about the extremely real Asteroid Belt.

8. Which of the following DID NOT happen before the naming of the Asteroid Belt?

- Ⓐ Mars was formed.
- Ⓑ Mercury was formed.
- Ⓒ Ceres was identified and named.
- Ⓓ Venus was formed.

9. What happened BEFORE the Asteroid Belt formed?

- Ⓐ The asteroid Ceres was named.
- Ⓑ The names of the Roman gods and goddesses were all used up.
- Ⓒ An asteroid the size of Texas was identified.
- Ⓓ The Earth was made

"Inventions have long since reached their limit." This was said by Julius Sextus Frontinus in AD 10. The Romans had invented aqueducts that could carry water for miles from lakes and rivers to dry places. Their engineers built roads that were so well-made that some of them still exist today. Their bridges spanned large distances. Frontinus decided that they had invented everything that could possibly be invented.

The patent office reviews new inventions to make sure that inventors are protected from those who might steal or copy their designs. The same statement made by Frontinus was later made by Charles H. Duell, who worked in the U.S. patent office in 1899. Telegraphs, phonographs, and steam engines had been invented. Mr. Duell became famous when he said, "Everything that can be invented has already been invented."

10. Why have the statements by Frontinus and Duell both become famous? Circle the correct answer.

    Ⓐ The statements are famous because they are similar.
    Ⓑ The statements are famous because they are different.
    Ⓒ The statements are famous because they are correct.
    Ⓓ The statements are famous because they are wrong.

In 218 B.C., Romans ruled most of the world that they knew about. They felt protected by the Alps – high, snow-covered mountains to the east and north of them that enemies would find very difficult to cross. Then Hannibal came from Carthage, in what is now North Africa, with 9000 infantrymen – soldiers on foot – and something even more surprising: elephants. Hannibal had crossed the Alps with 37 elephants – creatures so terrifying that the Romans, who had never seen such animals, were thrown into a panic.

11. Based on what you know in this passage, what do you predict happened next?

CHAPTER 2 → Lesson 4: Educational Expressions

1. What does carnivore mean in this paragraph?

Many animals in the wild eat other animals. These animals are called carnivores. Carnivores include lions, tigers, and bears.

- Ⓐ A plant eating animal
- Ⓑ An animal that eats plants and animals
- Ⓒ A meat eating animal
- Ⓓ An animal that eats dead

2. What is evaporation?

Clouds in the sky are able to produce rain. They get their water through evaporation. The sun heats the water in rivers, lakes, and even puddles, turning it into a vapor. Clouds are produced when lots of this vapor comes together.

- Ⓐ Water turning into rain.
- Ⓑ Clouds making rain.
- Ⓒ Water heating up and turning into a vapor.
- Ⓓ Water being absorbed by clouds.

3. What does the underlined word mean?

The world's <u>population</u> is growing every day! Thousands of babies are born each day, adding to the number of people on Earth.

- Ⓐ number of babies
- Ⓑ number of countries
- Ⓒ number of days
- Ⓓ number of people

4. What is the meaning of the underlined word?

My cousin Hans lives in Germany. He is a German <u>citizen</u>.

- Ⓐ person
- Ⓑ country
- Ⓒ A person living in a particular country
- Ⓓ visitor to a particular country

5. What is the meaning of the underlined word?

Because her country was at war, Marta's family decided to move to the United States. She and her family are <u>immigrants</u>.

Ⓐ people who move from a country
Ⓑ people who move to another country
Ⓒ people who are at war
Ⓓ people who are forced out of a country

6. What is the meaning of the underlined word?

I read an interesting story online today. The <u>setting</u> of the story is Mexico in 1870.

Ⓐ sitting
Ⓑ people in the story
Ⓒ the time and place the story occurred
Ⓓ cover of a book

7. What must the students do to come up with the sum?

My math teacher wrote five numbers on the board and asked the class to figure out the sum of the numbers.

Ⓐ subtract the numbers
Ⓑ add the numbers
Ⓒ divide the numbers
Ⓓ multiply the numbers

8. What is your teacher asking you to write?

After reading a book to the class, your teacher asks you to write a summary of the story.

Ⓐ A sentence about the main character.
Ⓑ The title of the book.
Ⓒ A few sentences describing what the story is about.
Ⓓ Your own story that is similar to the story she read.

Over the past 100 years, the Olympic games have endured. They remain a passion for fans, athletes, and trainers all over the world. While the love for this worldwide event is well-known, many changes have occurred since 1896.

In 1896, the Olympic games had 42 events and 245 competitors. These games were hosted in Athens, Greece. Only 14 nations were represented in those Olympic games. While only a little over one hundred years ago, women were not allowed to participate in the Olympic games. The most successful athlete from the 1896 games was a German wrestler/gymnast named Carl Schumann. Schumann won 4 gold medals.

The 2008 Olympic Games showed just how much a century can change things. Over 200 nations were represented in Beijing, China. There were over 10,000 males and females that competed for their chance at gold. A total of over 300 events were completed. Meanwhile, the most successful athlete from the 2008 games was American swimmer Michael Phelps. Phelps earned 8 gold medals in the 2008 Olympics. This was a new record for the most gold medals won during a single Olympic game. The 2008 Olympic games also marked an end for two popular events: baseball and softball.

While a lot has changed about the Olympic games, some things remain the same. The games are still held every four years. Additionally, the International Sports Federation Rules apply to the event. There are gold, silver, and bronze medals given today, just as they were 116 years ago in Athens, Greece.

9. **What does the underlined word in the following sentence from the passage above MOST LIKELY mean?**

   While a lot has changed about the Olympic games, some things <u>remain</u> the same.

   Ⓐ   change over time
   Ⓑ   stay the same
   Ⓒ   left over
   Ⓓ   new and exciting

10. **What does the underlined word in the following sentence from the passage above MOST LIKELY mean?**

    The 2008 Olympic games showed just how much a <u>century</u> can change things.

    Ⓐ   one year
    Ⓑ   five years
    Ⓒ   ten years
    Ⓓ   one hundred years

Simple Machines

Most of us don't go through our daily lives thinking about all the simple machines that we use, but they are everywhere. Without things like the lever, the wheel and axle, the pulley, the inclined plane, the wedge, and the screw, our lives would be much more complicated. Although simple machines have few parts, their function is to help maximize human strength and motion by using less force. As a result, there are six simple machines that make our lives easier.

Simple machines were created to make everyday tasks faster and less frustrating. Just think about how hard it would be to raise a flag without a pulley or how difficult loading a lawnmower on a trailer would be without the assistance of an inclined plane. Simple machines make jobs lighter.

Did you know that simple machines are used for fun activities too? Teeter-totters that allows children to move smoothly up and down use simple machines. Or picture the wheel and axle movement of your parents' steering wheel as you ride to and from the baseball field, the park, or a friend's birthday party.

These simple machines are also used to make some careers and <u>basic</u> tasks easier. An artist's job is made easier through the use of a wedge and chisel. They are able to use these simple machines when sculpting an image out of wood or clay. Additionally, a construction work might use a simple machine called a lever to drive nails into wood. Yes, to us this would be known as a hammer, but levers are nothing more than tools that aid in lifting or moving loads. A screw is an inclined plane that is wrapped around a pole to help hold objects together. This can be seen during the motion of turning a key in a lock.

The world around us uses these simple machines everywhere. Our lives are overflowing with uses for them. Next time, you walk through your home or enjoy a day at the park, take a moment to notice just how much these simple machines help us in our daily.

11. **What does the underlined word in the following sentence from the passage MOST LIKELY mean? Circle the correct answer choice.**

    These simple machines are also used to make some careers and <u>basic</u> tasks easier

    Ⓐ extra
    Ⓑ main
    Ⓒ really hard
    Ⓓ boring

Question 12 is based on the passage below

Amelia Earhart

Amelia Earhart was born on July 24, 1897. From that point forward, she was focused on earning a pilot's license. Holding on to that dream, she challenged herself with a variety of jobs to earn the $1,000 needed for flying lessons.

Soaring to new heights, Earhart proceeded to excel as a pilot. She received a medal from President Herbert Hoover in 1932 for her solo flight across the Atlantic. Meanwhile, she did not stop there. Earhart was the first female to fly from Hawaii to California.

Earhart's contribution to history ended on July 2, 1937 when a frantic message was received by the U. S. Coast Guard. Meanwhile, her devotion to creating change remains a <u>legacy</u>. This legacy emphasizes how setting dreams and achieving goals can be done through hard work and determination.

12. **What does the underlined word in the following sentence from the passage MOST LIKELY mean? Circle the correct answer choice.**

    Meanwhile, her devotion to creating change remains a <u>legacy</u>.

    Ⓐ plan
    Ⓑ wisdom
    Ⓒ gift
    Ⓓ problems

Question 13 is based on the passage below

Cell Phones in the Classroom

A familiar ringtone sounds out in the classroom directing everyone's attention to a shy student in the back row. Several years ago, this would have seemed a bit strange, but not today. A recent study showed that every one in three, third-grade students, has a cell phone. With so many students having access to these technology devices, a lot of talk has gone into whether to use them as learning tools or keep them banned from the classroom.

Let's think about their role as learning tools. Annie needs a calculator but forgot hers. She takes out her cell phone and can use the calculator app on the phone. Just across the room, Johnny is trying to spell the word "similar" so he uses the dictionary app on his phone to find the correct spelling. Another student in the class, Mitchell, has completed all of his work early, so he decides to use the multiplication app on his phone to review his multiplication facts in a fun and interactive way. These and other apps are making teachers and other school officials to see that cell phones do give students access to many resources that could actually save schools money.

While cell phones may sound great, not everyone is ready to lift the cell phone ban. There are still those that have major concerns. One concern is what to do about students that do not have a cell phone. Another worry is how to make sure students are using the phone as a learning tool instead of texting and social media. Additional concerns arise with how to address when a phone is broken or stolen while at school. Certainly, the list of problems that some schools have goes on and on.

The answer isn't clear for schools across the United States. Some schools are starting to lift the cell phone ban, but others are keeping it in place. As more and more backpacks get armed with cell phones, the discussion of having them in the classroom will certainly continue.

13. **What does the underlined word in the following sentence from the passage MOST LIKELY mean? Circle the correct answer choice.**

   These and other apps are making teachers and other school officials to see that cell phones do give students <u>access</u> to many resources that could actually save schools money.

   Ⓐ money
   Ⓑ a waste of time
   Ⓒ a block
   Ⓓ a connection

CHAPTER 2 → Lesson 5: Special Text Parts

Question 1 and 2 are based on the passage below

From McGuffey's Second Eclectic Reader

1. There are three kinds of bees: workers, drones, and queens.
2. Bees live in a house that is called a hive.
3. Only one queen can live in each hive. If she is lost or dead, the other bees will stop their work.
4. They are very wise and busy little creatures. They all join together to build cells of wax for their honey.
5.   Each bee takes its proper place, and does its own work. Some go out and gather honey from the flowers; others stay at home and work inside the hive.
6. The cells which they build are all one shape and size, and there are no spaces between them.
7. The cells are not round, but have six sides.
8. Have you ever looked into a glass hive to see the bees at work? They are always busy.
9. The drones do not work. Every year before winter, all of the drones are driven from the hive or killed. The reason the drones are driven from the hive or killed is because they did not help make the honey.
10. It is not safe for children to handle bees because they have stingers. Bees use their stingers as a great defensive tool.

1. How does the author of this selection help the reader easily locate information?

    Ⓐ By using a title
    Ⓑ By using headers
    Ⓒ By numbering the sentences
    Ⓓ By organizing the sentences

2. Which sentence tells the reader about the jobs bees perform?

    Ⓐ Sentence 3
    Ⓑ Sentence 4
    Ⓒ Sentence 6
    Ⓓ Sentence 9

With junk food becoming increasingly popular, and families being on the go more than ever, kids and their parents need to know how to make healthier food choices. It is important that children learn to make healthy food choices from an early age. If children learn to make these choices, it not only makes them healthy, but also it keeps them in shape.

Staying in shape is one way of saying that someone makes wise decisions about eating, exercising and maintaining a healthy weight. Staying in shape not only helps your body to work well, but helps you feel better too. Who doesn't want to feel well to enjoy fun activities with others?

While parents are responsible for making wise choices too, there are many ways that kids can step up to the plate and take charge. Let's start by talking about the types of foods that kids should eat. Sure, there are special occasions when a treat is in store, but fruits and vegetables should be a part of your daily food habits, not cake and ice cream. Your body needs a variety of healthy foods. By giving your body a lot of different foods, it will be able to get the nutrients that it needs. Don't be afraid to try new foods. You may not like everything that you try, but by trying new things, you will find more foods that you like. Throughout each day, try to eat five servings of fruits and vegetables. Hopefully, out of the five you will be able to find two fruits and three vegetables to enjoy.

Now that we have looked at some wise food choices, let's take a look at what you should be drinking. Water and milk are always the best choices. There is nothing that quenches your thirst like a cold glass of water. Now, you may have often wonder why schools serve cartons of milk. The truth is, milk is needed to help build strong bones because it contains calcium. Kids younger than 9 years old should drink 2 cups of milk per day. If milk isn't your favorite thing to drink, there are other ways to get the calcium that your body needs.

Some great dairy alternatives that introduce calcium into your diet are cheddar cheese and yogurt. You may be wondering if milk and water should be your only drink choices, and the answer is no. You can choose juice drinks that are 100% pure. This means that they are not loaded down with sugar. Many sodas, juice cocktails, and fruit punches have extraordinary amounts of sugar. Along with choosing the right foods and drinks, try to stay in shape with exercise.

It is important to try to find a way to be active for at least one hour daily. This might include playing basketball, riding a bike, or swimming. Now sometimes the weather won't allow you to enjoy these outdoor activities, so choose to get physical indoors by turning on some music that you enjoy and dancing to the beat. Other ideas include going bowling or turning your living room into a studio for "Simon Says" where you get to follow and give commands, such as: "Simon Says do 10 jumping jacks...." Just remember the idea is to get up and get active.

Staying fit doesn't have to be hard. It simply requires making wise choices. Try to make fruits, vegetables, milk, water, and exercise a part of your daily routine! You will feel great, and your body will thank you by giving you lots of energy to do the things that you most enjoy.

3. **If the author of this passage wanted the reader to do additional research, what key word would BEST help them in their Internet search?**

Ⓐ Jumping Jacks
Ⓑ Ways to Stay Healthy
Ⓒ Drinking Milk and Water
Ⓓ The Food Group

4. **What type of picture WOULD NOT help to make the information in this passage clearer?**

Ⓐ The Food Pyramid
Ⓑ A chart showing types of exercise for kids
Ⓒ A chart showing fruits and vegetables
Ⓓ Favorite junk foods

Question 5 is based on the passage below

Good Manners Can Help You

Good manners can be seen at home, at school, on the playground, and at the dining table where we eat our meals. A well mannered person is polite and gentle when talking.

Everyone likes a person who is polite and good mannered. Good manners are always liked by everyone and after can bring good rewards.

Therefore, we should always remember to do what is right.

All that is wrong displeases everyone. Therefore, we should not do what is wrong. Often, we will be rewarded for our good actions.

Children who consistently come late to school are not dependable. It is difficult to provide important work for them. These children could even lose some friends.

All of us make mistakes. When we make a mistake, we do not like to be punished. We like to be forgiven. Therefore, we, too, should forgive the mistakes of others. Forgiveness is a great virtue.

It is easy to make a mistake, but it is not easy to forget that mistake. When we make a mistake, we should feel sorry about it. We also apologize to the person whom we have hurt.

We should not cheat on an examination. Cheating always does more harm than good. We can choose out friends wisely.

5. What part of this selection gives the reader a clue to know what they will be reading about?

Ⓐ the second sentence
Ⓑ the header
Ⓒ the title
Ⓓ the italics

Question 6 and 7 are based on the passage below

The Amazon Rainforest

The Amazon Rainforest is full of life. It has sounds of all kinds, water rushing and falling, and animals communicating. It's a busy place where animals are looking for food, trying to survive, and looking to expand their families. The Amazon Rainforest in South America, has one tiny animal that is almost completely camouflaged from the rest of the animals, except for one small body part: its bright red eyes!

This animal is known as the Red-Eyed Tree Frog. It lives deep in the tall trees in the Amazon. It resides mostly in South America, it can also be found in Central America and parts of Mexico.

Many bright colors decorate the body of the adult Red-Eyed Tree frog. Its main color is green, with a mixture of yellow, orange, and blue on its belly. The frog can change its colors based on its feelings or needs; the color often changes from green to reddish-brown. Its toes have suction cups that help the Red-Eyed Tree Frog attach itself to the environment. The suction cups give the frog traction to stand firm on wet leaves. Its legs are built better for climbing than for swimming, and it is almost never on the ground. It keeps jumping around steadily pace from tree to tree.

The physical properties of the Red-Eyed Tree Frog also makes it different, and helps it survive. Unlike most humans, or even other animals, the male frog is actually smaller than the female. Male frogs only reach around two inches in length while the females can grow to be three inches. The RedEyed Tree Frog is also a carnivore. The tree frog eats grasshoppers, moths, and other insects. However, it eats smaller frogs, too! It is known to eat almost anything that can fit in its mouth.

Many people find it fascinating to know that the red eyes are not just for looks; they help the frogs survive. In fact, the red eyes scare other animals easily and help these frogs escape from their predators. With their greenish color skin, they tend to blend in with their surroundings. When they sleep, they are virtually invisible. However, if other animals see them and try to attack, the Red-Eyed Tree Frog will open its wide, red eyes, and the predators, which usually consist of snakes, birds, or bats, will scurry away. In many cases, the predators may also be stunned into stillness at the sight of the red eyes, long enough for the frog to escape.

The Red-Eyed Tree frog is a unique animal that is able to protect itself even though it is very small. With deadly predators and a dangerous environment surrounding it, the frog relies on camouflage, and its bright red eyes to scare off unwanted guests and enemies.

6. **What would be a better title for this selection?**

    Ⓐ The Amazing Red-Eyed Tree Frog
    Ⓑ The Animals of the Amazon Rainforest
    Ⓒ Where to Find the Amazon Rainforest
    Ⓓ The Endangered Amazon Rainforest

7. **What text feature would help the reader better understand the third paragraph in this selection?**

    Ⓐ A map of the Amazon rainforest
    Ⓑ A diagram of the tree frog
    Ⓒ A photograph of the tree frog
    Ⓓ An illustration of where the tree frog lives

Question 8 and 9 are based on the passage below

Matter is everything that surrounds you on a daily basis. There are five primary states of matter. Matter is made of atoms and molecules, mass, and takes up any amount of space. There are five states that matter can be found in: solid, liquid, gas, plasma, and Bose-Einstein condensate; but, the main states are solid, gas, and liquid. It is possible for matter to move from one state to another. One example of this is water. In its liquid form, we can put water in a cup and drink it. Water can also be found in a solid form which is ice, or in a gas form which is fog.

8. **What would be an appropriate heading title for this section of text?**

    Ⓐ Matter
    Ⓑ Space
    Ⓒ Atoms
    Ⓓ Objects

9. **Which of the following could be included to improve the information provided in this passage?**

    Ⓐ a picture of space
    Ⓑ a picture of water as a solid, liquid, and a gas
    Ⓒ a picture of rain
    Ⓓ a diagram of an atom

10. This poem is meant to be read out loud. Why does the author use apostrophes (') in this selection?

from McGuffey's Second Eclectic Reader
blos'soms drear'y wea'ry pinks smell'ing toil'ing
lev'ies buzz fra'grant this'tle weeds scent
treas'ure yel'low mead'ow tax sum'mer clo'ver
cloud'y dai'sy daf'fo dil lies columbine humming

Ⓐ To show the reader how to pronounce the words
Ⓑ To show the reader where the syllables divide in the words
Ⓒ To show the reader the meaning of each word
Ⓓ To show the reader how loudly to read the selection

CHAPTER 2 → Lesson 6: What Did You Already Know?

Question 1 is based on the passage below

Everything in nature follows a pattern. Circles, lines, spirals, and angles are repeated to make a design or a pattern. Patterns in nature are not just pretty adornments. They serve a purpose that has helped nature survive and flourish.

Have you ever taken a close look at a beehive? Well, not too close or you might get stung! The natural pattern in beehives is so perfect that it seems to be computer designed. The hives are made up of layers and layers of cells. Each cell has six perfectly equal sides or hexagons. Why would bees build six-sided cells, instead of round, or box shaped ones? The reason is that the bee is a genius at geometry and architecture! Six-sided cells use up every bit of space and allow bees to get the maximum area for storing honey. Also, Hexagons use the least honeycomb wax because all six sides are identical in length. The bees don't waste space, material, or effort. Aren't they smart insects?

1. Where might a reader use the information about hexagons from this passage?

Ⓐ When solving a math problem on algebra.
Ⓑ When writing a math paper on geometric properties of a hexagon.
Ⓒ When building your home.
Ⓓ None of the above.

Question 2 is based on the passage below

What is the most poisonous creature on Earth? Many people guess that the answer would be a snake, a jellyfish, a scorpion, or a spider. Actually, most scientists agree that the most venomous animal is a harmless-looking small golden frog, called "teribilis." The golden frog is so toxic that even touching it can be dangerous to humans. A single frog contains enough poison to kill 20,000 mice or ten people.

2. What should you do if you see a teribilis? Write your answer in the box below.

The Bluegrass State

There is one state with water, wildlife, and mountains. Does this sound too good to be true? Well, it isn't all of these natural features are in The Bluegrass State. These are some of the reasons that people visit Kentucky. Kentucky is home to wonderful lakes that offer fun water activities.

Cumberland Falls is a huge waterfall. It has been nicknamed "the Niagara of the South". If you are looking to do more than just see the water, a visit to beautiful Lake Cumberland might be a good stop for you. Here you can enjoy boating, fishing, or jet skiing. The Bluegrass State has a lot to offer for those looking for fun in the water.

Maybe, you are more of a wildlife person. Many people love hunting in the western part of the state. Natural wildlife can be found throughout the area. There are excursions in the Daniel Boone National Forest that are great also.

If this does not sound like fun to you, then you might like to learn more about Kentucky's horses. You can visit one of the race tracks or horse farms. Visitors from all over the world have visited Churchill Downs. Their horses race in the Kentucky Derby. Several other races that can be attended throughout the year. Other locations that allow you to enjoy Kentucky's best thoroughbreds include the Kentucky Horse Park and Keeneland.

Kentucky's tourism doesn't stop there. Guests can visit Mammoth Cave and the home of Abraham Lincoln. Certainly, the Bluegrass State is filled with features that keep people visiting this beautiful state.

3. **Based on the author's description of Kentucky, what type of person might NOT enjoy visiting Kentucky?**

   Ⓐ a hiker
   Ⓑ a horse lover
   Ⓒ a person who loves shopping
   Ⓓ a camper

The ostrich is the largest bird in the world, but it cannot fly. Its legs are so strong and long that it can travel faster by running. Ostriches use their wings to help them gather speed when they start to run. They also use them as brakes when they are turning and stopping.

Ostriches have been known to run at a rate of 96 km an hour. This is faster than horses can run, and as fast as most people drive a car. These huge birds stand as tall as a horse and sometimes weigh as much as 135 kg. In Africa, their home continent, they are often seen with large animals. The zebra, which is also a fast runner, seems to be one of their favorite companions.

Each ostrich egg weighs as much as two dozen chicken eggs. Ostrich eggs are delicious to eat and are often used as food in Africa. The shells also are made into cups and ornaments.

4. What does the author of this article assume the reader knows before reading the passage?

Ⓐ What an ostrich looks like
Ⓑ What horses look like
Ⓒ How heavy chicken eggs are
Ⓓ Where ostriches live

Question 5 is based on the passage below

Amelia Earhart was born on July 24, 1897. She lived with her grandparents until the age of 12 when she and her sister went to live with their parents in 1909. Amelia's plans were to attend college, but when she came across four wounded World War I soldiers, she decided that she wanted to become a nurse. Her dedication to helping people led her from nursing to work as a social worker. While she worked as a social worker, she often spent her free time teaching immigrant children how to speak English.

Her most noteworthy journey began in 1920 when she took a ten-minute plane ride that completely changed her life. She decided to focus on earning a pilot's license. She challenged herself with a variety of jobs to earn the $1,000 needed for flying lessons to fulfill her dream.

Amelia Earhart proceeded to excel as a pilot. She received a medal from President Herbert Hoover in 1932 for her solo flight across the Atlantic. She did not stop there. Earhart was the first female to fly from Hawaii to California.

Amelia Earhart's contribution to history ended on July 2, 1937, when a frantic message was received by the U. S. Coast Guard. The message was from Earhart stating that she and the plane were in trouble. The plane went down, and no one has ever seen Earhart again. Her devotion to creating change remains a legacy. This legacy emphasizes how setting dreams and achieving goals can be done through hard work and determination.

5. How might some readers disagree with the author's opinion in this passage?

Ⓐ Some might believe that Earhart was not a pilot.
Ⓑ Some might disagree with Earhart's choice to not attend college.
Ⓒ Some readers might think that Earhart DID NOT leave a legacy behind.
Ⓓ Some readers might think that Earhart did not live during World War II.

Cell Phones in the Classroom

A familiar ringtone sounds in the classroom directing everyone's attention to a shy student in the back row. Several years ago, this would have seemed a bit strange, but not today. A recent study showed that one in three third-grade students have a cell phone. With so many students having access to technology devices, a lot of talks have gone into deciding whether to use them as learning tools or to ban them from the classroom.

Let's think about cell phones' role as learning tools. Annie needs a calculator but forgot hers. She takes out her cell phone and can use the calculator app on the phone. Just across the room, Johnny is trying to spell the word "similar," so he uses the dictionary app on his phone to find the correct spelling. Mitchell, has completed all of his work early, so he decides to use the multiplication app on his phone to review multiplication facts in a fun and interactive way. These devices are causing teachers and other school officials to see that cell phones give students access to resources that actually save schools money.

While cell phones may sound great, not every school district is ready to lift the cell phone ban. There are still those that have major concerns. One concern is what to do about students who do not have a cell phone. Another worry is how to make sure students are using the phone as a learning tool instead of texting and social media. Additional concerns arise with how to address when a phone is broken or stolen while at school. Certainly, the list of problems that some schools have goes on and on.

The answer isn't clear for schools across the United States. Some schools are starting to lift the cell phone ban, but others are keeping it in place. As students pack backpacks with cell phones, the discussion of having them in the classroom will certainly continue.

6. **If a parent responded to this passage by saying that their child was spending too much time texting in class, what is their point of view regarding this author's passage?**

   Ⓐ They agree with him entirely.
   Ⓑ The parent dislikes the author.
   Ⓒ They think that cell phones should be banned from the classroom.
   Ⓓ They think that parents should be able to make this choice, not schools.

The Asteroid Belt

It's shaped like a doughnut, made from lumps of rock, and looks like a pattern of floating rocks moving in a circle. This strange sounding object is the Asteroid Belt. The Asteroid Belt was formed from lumps of rock left over after other planets formed. Yes, it is shaped like a doughnut and can be found between the orbits of Mars and Jupiter. The Asteroid Belt has two layers. The inner layer has asteroids made of metals. The outer layer has rocky asteroids.

When you look at the Asteroid Belt it looks like floating rocks moving in a circle. Scientists say that there are millions of asteroids in this belt. It may sound pretty funny, but scientists say that there is still a lot of empty space. As you have probably already guessed, the Asteroid Belt is pretty big. It is actually 215 million miles wide. Jupiter keeps the asteroids inside the belt and prevents them from hitting the planets in space. Jupiter's gravity is what holds the asteroids in place.

The chunks of rock inside of the belt were named asteroid, meaning star and rock. The first asteroids seen in the belt were named after gods and heroes. The first largest asteroid found was named Ceres after a Roman goddess. Ceres was discovered on January 1, 1801. It is the size of Texas, and is it called a dwarf planet. Before an asteroid is named, a group of people check to make sure it is not an inappropriate name. Now that most Roman hero names have been used up, scientists are using the name of the astrophysicist to name an asteroid. A lot of information remains unknown about the extremely real Asteroid Belt.

7. How might someone most successfully disagree with the author of this passage?

Ⓐ   A reader might think that the world does not date back millions of years.
Ⓑ   The reader might argue that there are no other planets besides Earth.
Ⓒ   The reader might believe that there are no such things as asteroids.
Ⓓ   The reader might believe that the Earth is an asteroid.

From McGuffey's Second Eclectic Reader "Yes, we're busy night and day,

As o'er the earth we take our way.
We are bearers of the rain
To the grasses, and flowers, and grain;
We guard you from the sun's bright rays,
In the sultry summer days."

8. What is most likely the "we" described in this poem?

Ⓐ birds
Ⓑ trees
Ⓒ clouds
Ⓓ rivers

Let the Adventure Begin...

There is nothing better than hopping in the car or on a plane and setting off for an adventure. Adults and children alike love exploring new places. Now, sometimes this desire for adventure can leave parents and kids disagreeing about where to go. Let's take a look at some places that are sure to make everyone happy.

Who wouldn't love spending some time at the Grand Canyon? This type of trip may take some planning, but it is sure to be worth it. Families can enjoy looking at the Grand Canyon from a glass-bottom observation deck that extends about 70 feet over the West Rim of the Canyon. Did I also mention that you will be 4,000 feet above the Colorado River?

Another hot spot for families to visit is the Redwood National Park in California. Now, looking at the ancient, skyscraper high sequoias is quite breath-taking, but leave some excitement for the cool aquatic life that can be experienced in this area. There are underwater creatures such as orange and purple ochre sea stars and green anemones that can be explored during one of the free summer tide pool tours available at the Redwood National Park.

If geographically, you desire a location closer to the East Coast, consider checking out Monticello in Virginia. Here, families can enjoy viewing Thomas Jefferson's estate. There is even the Griffin Discovery Room where everything can be touched. That's right – everything! Kids can enjoy touching replicas of Jefferson's most prized possessions, including his alcove bed and his polygraph machine. There are also clothes that were modeled after the third President's sense of style for kids to try on and role play in.

Don't worry if you are the northern part of the country, your family might enjoy the Craters of the Moon National Monument in Preserve. This Idaho attraction is "the only official weird park" in the country. There is a jagged, black landscape that was molded by volcanic eruptions that date back 15,000 years ago. There is even a 618-square mile lava field. You won't find another one of those in the United States.

Sure, the discussion of great places to visit could go on, but don't you have somewhere to go? Pack your bags and start discovering some of nature's beauty that awaits you all across the United States.

9. **Which of the following people would DISAGREE with the information provided by the author of this passage? Circle the correct answer choice.**

    Ⓐ A person who has visited all seven continents
    Ⓑ Someone that only enjoys traveling to locations close to their home
    Ⓒ Someone that hates traveling
    Ⓓ Someone that only enjoys historical tourist attractions

10. **Which of the following statements is a FACT?**

    Ⓐ Idaho has the only official weird park in the United States.
    Ⓑ Monticello, Virginia has beautiful scenery.
    Ⓒ If you love history, you will love visiting Jefferson's home.
    Ⓓ The Grand Canyon is the most beautiful sight in the United States.

Question 11 is based on the passage below

PATTY AND THE SQUIRREL
from McGuffey's Second Eclectic Reader

1. Little Patty lives in a log house near a great forest. She has no sisters, and her big brothers are away all day helping their father.

2. But Patty is never lonely; for, though the nearest house is miles away, she has many little friends. There are two squirrels that live in the woods that are her friends.

3. How did Patty teach them to be so tame? Patty came to the woods often, and was always so quiet and gentle that the squirrels soon found they need not be afraid of her.

4. She brought her bread and milk to eat under the trees, and was sure to leave crumbs for the squirrels.

5. When they came near, she sat very still and watched them. So, little by little, she made them her friends, till, at last, they would sit on her shoulder, and eat from her hand.

6. Patty even helps the squirrels build their summer and winter homes. Their summer homes are made of leaves, and sticks, and moss. Their winter homes are found in hollow old trees.

7. Patty helps the squirrels and the squirrels help Patty not be lonely.

11. What do you think caused Patty to befriend the squirrels?

CHAPTER 2 → Lesson 7: Informational Illustrations

Question 1 and 2 are based on the information below

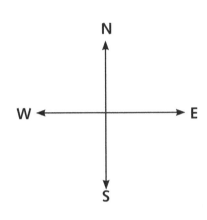

Elizabeth recently moved to Riverville. She is having a hard time finding her way around town.

1. What direction will Elizabeth have to travel in order to get to Mill Street?

Ⓐ South
Ⓑ East
Ⓒ North
Ⓓ There is not a Mill Street listed on this map.

2. If Elizabeth leaves River Street walking west what streets will she travel to get to the school?

Ⓐ Main, Oak, Pine, Maple, School
Ⓑ River, Hill, Grove, School
Ⓒ River, Maple, School
Ⓓ River, Maple, Lemon, Pine

There are eight named planets in our solar system. The planets orbit the sun at their own pace. Mercury takes 87.969 days to make a complete trip around the sun. Neptune makes the longest journey around the sun. It takes this planet 60,190 days to make a trip around the sun. Neptune is the farthest planet from the sun; this is the reason for the extended travel time. Despite the placement of the planets each one has to orbit the sun.

Orbiting Times around the Sun

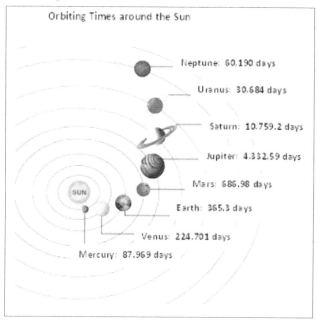

Orbiting Times around the Sun

Neptune: 60,190 days

Uranus: 30.684 days

Saturn: 10.759.2 days

Jupiter: 4.332.59 days

Mars: 686.98 days

Earth: 365.3 days

Venus: 224.701 days

Mercury: 87.969 days

SUN

3. Which planets take fewer days than Earth to orbit the sun?

(A) Mars, Jupiter, Saturn, Uranus, Neptune
(B) Earth takes the fewest days to orbit the sun.
(C) Venus and Mercury
(D) Neptune and Uranus

4. From the passage and the illustration, what would be the climate difference between Mars and Uranus?

(A) Mars' climate is colder than Uranus.
(B) Uranus' climate is warmer than Mars.
(C) There is no difference in the two planets' climates.
(D) Mars' climate is warmer than Uranus.

5. From the passage and the illustration, what would be the climate difference between Neptune and Jupiter?

Question 6 is based on the information below

Primates

There are more than 300 species of primates identified by scientists. There are three major categories of primates. These three categories are: apes, monkeys, and prosimians. Apes are generally larger than the other two categories of primates. The smallest primate is a pygmy mouse lemur and the largest is a gorilla. Apes, monkeys, and prosimians can be found on the continents of Africa and Asia. Additionally, some species of monkeys can be found in the wild in Central and South America.

6. After reading the story and viewing the map, where can you find primates in the wild?

- Ⓐ North America, Central America, South America, Europe, Asia, Africa, and Australia
- Ⓑ Central and South America only
- Ⓒ Primates are found on every continent in the wild.
- Ⓓ Central America, South America, Africa, and Asia

Primates

There are three basic categories of primates. These three categories are apes, monkeys, and prosimians. There are distinct differences in apes, monkeys, and prosimians. For instance, each primate has a unique nose shape. Apes have hook shaped noses that are dry, monkeys have flat noses that are dry, and prosimians have dog-like snouts that are always wet. Additionally, they are dissimilar in the number of species that have been identified. Scientists have acknowledged that there are approximately 23 species of apes, hundreds of species of monkeys, and about 50 species of prosimians. Further, differences in the three categories of primates are the lifespan of each. Apes can live to be sixty years old, whereas prosimians generally only live to be nineteen. Monkeys have been known to live up to thirty years. A final contrast is when the different primates are most active. Apes and monkeys are more active during the day while prosimians are more active at night. As you can see these three categories of primates have distinct differences

Types of Primates	Apes	Monkeys	Prosimians
Nose	Hook Shaped and Dry	Flat Nosed and Dry	Dog-like Snout and Wet
Number of Species	23	Hundreds	50
Lifespan	Up to 60 years	Up to 30 years	Up to 19 years
Time of Activity	Diurnal (during the day)	Diurnal (during the day)	Nocturnal (at night)

7. Part A
Which two facts do apes and monkeys have in common?

Ⓐ They both have dry noses and are active during the day.
Ⓑ They have the same number of identified species.
Ⓒ There are no similarities between monkeys and apes.
Ⓓ They have similar lifespans and their noses are the same shape.

Part B
What is one of the differences between the prosimians and monkeys?

Ⓐ There are no noted differences between prosimians and monkeys.
Ⓑ They are both larger than most apes.
Ⓒ Monkeys have hundreds of species that have been identified and there are only eighty species of prosimians identified.
Ⓓ Prosimians have a lifespan of only nineteen years and monkeys can live up to thirty years.

Question 8 and 9 are based on the passage below

Ice cream has become a popular treat for many Americans.

The United States of America consumes more ice cream in one year than any other country. The average American eats forty-eight pints of ice cream a year. The most common flavor is vanilla. July has been deemed National Ice Cream Month in the United States. Since Americans love ice cream so much it might be important to examine the history of ice cream in the U.S.

Ice cream was first introduced in the United States in the 1700s. Only the wealthy could afford to buy it. The first widely seen advertisement for ice cream was circulated in 1777. The ice cream industry began in Boston in 1851. The ice cream sundae was created in 1874. The first ice cream cone was in 1904 at the St. Louis World's Fair.

Early 1700s	1777	1851	1874	1904
Ice Cream was introduced in the U.S.	Ice cream was first advertised in the U.S.	Ice cream industry began in Boston	The ice cream sundae was invented	The ice cream cone were invented at the World's Fair in St. Louis

8. **In which year was ice cream first advertised in the United States? Circle the correct answer choice.**

   Ⓐ 1904
   Ⓑ 1851
   Ⓒ Early 1700s
   Ⓓ 1777

9. **What two ice cream events occurred during the 1800s?**

   Ⓐ Ice cream was introduced in America and the ice cone was invented.
   Ⓑ The ice cream sundae and the ice cream cone were invented.
   Ⓒ The ice cream industry began in Boston and the first ice cream sundae was invented.
   Ⓓ Ice cream was introduced in the U.S. and it was first advertised.

CHAPTER 2 → Lesson 8: Connect the Dots

Question 1 is based on the passage below

The ostrich is the largest bird in the world, but it cannot fly. Its legs are so strong and long that it can travel faster by running. Ostriches use their wings to help them gather speed when they start to run. They also use them as brakes when they are turning and stopping.

Ostriches have been known to run at a rate of 96 km an hour. This is faster than horses can run, and as fast as most people drive a car. These huge birds stand as tall as a horse and sometimes weigh as much as 135 kg. In Africa, their home continent, they are often seen with large animals. The zebra, which is also a fast runner, seems to be one of their favorite companions.

Each ostrich egg weighs as much as two dozen chicken eggs. Ostrich eggs are delicious to eat and are often used as food in Africa. The shells also are made into cups and ornaments.

1. What is the author's opinion of the ostrich?

 Ⓐ The author does not find it interesting.
 Ⓑ The author finds the ostrich extraordinary.
 Ⓒ The author likes ostrich eggs.
 Ⓓ The author likes zebras.

Questions 2-6 is based on the passage below

Everything in nature follows a pattern. Circles, lines, spirals, and angles are repeated to make a pattern. Patterns in nature are not just pretty adornments. They serve a purpose that has helped nature survive and flourish. Have you ever taken a close look at a beehive? (Well, not too close or you might get stung!) The natural pattern in beehives is so perfect that it seems to be computer designed. The hives are made up of layers and layers of cells. Each cell has six perfectly equal sides. Why would bees build hexagonal cells, why not circular or box-shaped ones? The bee is a genius at geometry and architecture! Six-sided cells allow bees to get maximum space for storing honey. Hexagons also use the least building material because all six sides are common to other cells. The bees don't waste space, material or effort. Aren't they smart insects?

2. Based on the selection, what is likely to happen to you if you go near a beehive?

 Ⓐ You will be stung.
 Ⓑ You will eat honey.
 Ⓒ You will be worried.
 Ⓓ You will get hurt.

3. What can you conclude after reading this passage?

- (A) Hexagon shaped buildings use more building materials.
- (B) Bees are very smart insects.
- (C) Nothing in nature follows a pattern.
- (D) Bees are lazy.

4. Based on this passage, which of the following statements is true?

- (A) The above passage can be used to write a paper on nature and bees.
- (B) The above passage can be referred to while writing a paper on hornets.
- (C) The above passage can be used while writing a paper on spiders.
- (D) The above passage can be used while writing a paper on how not to waste space.

5. Where might a reader use the information about hexagons from this passage?

- (A) When solving a math problem on algebra.
- (B) When writing a math paper on geometric properties of a hexagon.
- (C) When building your home.
- (D) None of the above.

6. Why does the author ask, "Have you ever taken a close look at a beehive"?

- (A) The author wants to know whether you have seen a beehive.
- (B) The author likes the beehives.
- (C) The author wants to introduce us to beehives and the way they look.
- (D) The author does not like the look of the beehives.

Question 7 is based on the passage below

THE BEE from McGuffey's Second Eclectic Reader

1. There are three kinds of bees: workers, drones, and queens.
2. Bees live in a house that is called a hive.
3. Only one queen can live in each hive. If she is lost or dead, the other bees will stop their work.
4. They are very wise and busy little creatures. They all join together to build cells of wax for their honey.
5. Each bee takes its proper place, and does its own work. Some go out and gather honey from the flowers; others stay at home and work inside the hive.
6. The cells which they build are all of one shape and size, and no room is left between them.
7. The cells are not round, but have six sides.
8. Have you ever looked into a glass hive to see the bees while at work? They are always busy.
9. The drones do not work. Every year before winter, all the drones are driven from the hive or killed. The reason the drones are driven from the hive or killed is because they did not help make the honey.

10. It is not safe for children to handle bees because they have stingers. Bees use their stingers as a great defensive tool.

7. Based on this selection, what are you LEAST likely to see a worker bee doing?

Ⓐ Building a six-sided hive
Ⓑ Gathering honey from a flower
Ⓒ Sitting still
Ⓓ Stinging a child who is holding it

8. Which of the following types of writing will Annie be completing?

Annie is writing a speech about the effects of second-hand tobacco smoke. She is going to present this to the members of the city council at their monthly meeting.

Ⓐ An opinion piece
Ⓑ An autobiography piece
Ⓒ A narrative piece
Ⓓ A poetry reading

9. Which of the following types of writing did Jose compose?

Jose wrote an interesting passage about the similarities and differences between flies and mosquitos.

Ⓐ An opinion piece
Ⓑ An informational piece
Ⓒ A narrative piece
Ⓓ A fictional short story

10. Which type of writing is Michael using to complete the PowerPoint?

Michael just returned from the Dominican Republic. He is creating a Powerpoint presentation about his exciting trip to share with the class, it is complete with pictures and descriptions.

Ⓐ An opinion piece
Ⓑ An informational piece
Ⓒ A narrative piece
Ⓓ A fictional short story

With junk food becoming increasingly popular and families being on the go more than ever, kids and their parents need to know how to make healthier choices. It is important that children learn to make healthy choices from an early age. If children learn to make these choices it not only makes them healthy but also it keeps them in shape.

Staying in shape is one way of saying that someone makes wise decisions about what they eat, have active exercise routines, and is able to stay at a healthy weight. Staying in shape not only helps your body to work well, but you will feel better too. Who doesn't want to feel well enough to enjoy fun activities with the people around us?

While parents are responsible for making wise choices too, there are many ways that kids can step up to the plate and take charge. Let's start by talking about the types of foods that kids should eat. Sure, there are special occasions when a treat is in store, but fruits and vegetables should be a part of your daily foods, not cake and ice cream. Your body needs a variety of healthy foods. By giving your body a lot of different foods, it will be able to get the nutrients that it needs. Don't be afraid to try new foods. You may not like everything that you try, but by trying new things, you will find more and more foods that you do like. Throughout each day, try to eat five servings of fruits and vegetables. Hopefully, out of those five you will be able to find two fruits and three vegetables to enjoy.

Now, that we have looked at some wise food choices, let's take a look at what you should be drinking. Water and milk are always the best choices. There is nothing that quenches your thirst like a cold glass of water. Now, you may have often wondered why schools offer up cartons of milk. Truth is, milk is needed to help build strong bones because it contains calcium. Kids younger than 9 years old should drink 2 cups of milk per day. If milk isn't your favorite thing to drink there are other ways to get the calcium that your body needs. Some great alternatives to introduce calcium into your diet is cheddar cheese and yogurt.

You may be wondering if milk and water should be your only drink choices, and the answer is no. Choose juice drinks that are 100% pure. This means that they are not loaded down with sugars the way that sodas, juice cocktails, and fruit punches are. Choosing to drink and eat right is one step towards staying in shape, but you also need to get exercise!

It is important to try to find a way to be active for at least one hour daily. This might include playing basketball, riding a bike, or swimming. Now sometimes the weather won't allow you to enjoy these outdoor activities, so choose to get physical indoors by turning on some music that you enjoy and dancing to the beat. Other ideas include going bowling or turning your living room into a studio for "Simon Says" where you get to follow and give commands, such as: "Simon Says do 10 jumping jacks...." Just remember the idea is get up and get active.

Staying fit doesn't have to be hard. It simply requires making wise choices. Make fruits, vegetables, milk, water, and exercise a part of your daily routine! You will feel great, and your body will thank you by giving you lots of energy to do the things that you most enjoy.

11. What was the author's purpose for including facts in this passage?

12. Which of the following organizational techniques BEST describes how the author wrote this passage? Choose the correct answer by circling it.

Ⓐ In the order that things happened
Ⓑ Showing causes and effects for making healthy lifestyle choices
Ⓒ Telling the events that created someone's opinion about junk food
Ⓓ Telling memories from the author's life about his experiences with food

Question 13 and 14 are based on the passage below

It's the Twenty-First Century

With new times comes change. Allowing cell phones in classrooms is one type of change that I am talking about. So many kids have them, so why not let them be used for something good?

If we were allowed to use cell phones in class, we wouldn't have to always be waiting for the computer lab to open up. We can use our cell phones to do research.

Our teachers love showing us cool learning tools, but we never get to use them during the school day. Sometimes we forget about them before we go home. If we have our cell phones right there in class, we can use them then and not forget about what we are being shown.

Cell phones can also replace planners. They can allow us to keep track of important due dates for assignments, the days tests are scheduled, and other important reminders. Students lose their assignment books, but they will keep up with their cell phones.

I hope that I have shown you why having cell phones in the classroom is a great idea. This resource can benefit all of us. Let's lift that cell phone ban. After all, it is the twenty-first century.

13. What was the author's reason for writing this piece? Circle the correct answer choice.

    Ⓐ To state an opinion
    Ⓑ To narrate a memory
    Ⓒ To inform about the history of cell phones
    Ⓓ To entertain the reader with a fictional story

14. Why does the author MOST LIKELY end the first paragraph with a question? Circle the correct answer choice.

    Ⓐ He wants the reader to stop what they are doing and go research the answer.
    Ⓑ He wants to make the reader pause and think.
    Ⓒ He wants to make sure that all readers agree with his opinion.
    Ⓓ He wants to take up space with one extra sentence.

CHAPTER 2 → Lesson 9: Compare and Contrast Important Points and Key Details

Questions 1-3 are based on the passage below

Louisiana

It has been said that the state of Louisiana is a melting pot of people. Many different ethnic groups have settled into pockets of this great state. Not only are there Vietnamese, Spanish, and Europeans, but there are also two unique ethnic groups. These two groups are the Cajuns and the Creoles. The Cajuns are the French Canadians that moved down from Canada to Southern Louisiana. They fled Canada because of a British imposed rule that attempted to force all Canadians to accept the King's Protestant religion. Most of the French Canadians who moved to Louisiana were Catholics. When the Cajuns arrived in Louisiana they were accepted and allowed to practice any religion. As the Cajuns became more settled in Louisiana their customs and heritage began to impact the current populations' way of life. The Cajuns impact is still seen today throughout Louisiana.

Louisiana

The state of Louisiana has a mix of people from many different backgrounds. Many ethnic groups have settled into different parts of the state. There are people from Vietnam, Canada, and European countries that call this great state home. Additionally, there are two groups that moved into Louisiana many years ago. These two groups are the Creoles and Cajuns. It can be said these two groups of people have a blended set of backgrounds.

The Creoles are defined as any person who was born in New Orleans that has French or Spanish family roots. This includes anyone that comes from Africa, the Caribbean, France, or any Spanish country. The Creoles, like the Cajuns, have had a huge impact on the Louisiana lifestyle. Many of their traditions have contributed to Louisiana's unique art, music, and cooking. New Orleans is truly a different place to live and visit thanks to the Cajuns and the Creoles.

1. **From the two passages, which of the following answer choices explain a similarity between the Cajuns and the Creoles?**

   Ⓐ Cajuns and Creoles both moved to Louisiana from Canada.
   Ⓑ Both Cajuns and Creoles fled to Louisiana because they were Catholic and were not allowed to practice their religion in their home countries.
   Ⓒ All Cajuns and Creoles came from Spanish speaking countries.
   Ⓓ Both Cajuns and Creoles have impacted the Louisiana lifestyle.

2. **Which of the following answer choices accurately describe a difference in the two passages?**

   Ⓐ Cajuns fled Canada because they were not allowed to practice the Catholic religion. Creoles are people who live in New Orleans and are from French or Spanish family roots.
   Ⓑ Cajuns only live in New Orleans and Creoles live in only Southern Louisiana.
   Ⓒ There are no differences between Cajuns and Creoles because they are the same people.
   Ⓓ Cajuns are mainly from Africa while, Creoles are from Canada.

3. **Which of the following answer choices accurately describe a key detail of these passages?**

   Ⓐ A key point of these passages is that Louisiana offers many different types of food.
   Ⓑ A key point of these passages is that a lot of people have moved from Canada to Louisiana.
   Ⓒ A key point of these passages is that Cajuns and Creoles have impacted the Louisiana way of life.
   Ⓓ A key point of these passages is that you should visit Louisiana on your next vacation.

> **Question 4 and 5 are based on the passage below**

Cell Phones in the Classroom

A familiar ringtone sounds in the classroom directing everyone's attention to a shy student in the back row. Several years ago, this would have seemed a bit strange, but not today. A recent study showed that one in three third-grade students have a cell phone. With so many students having access to technology devices, a lot of talks have gone into deciding whether to use them as learning tools or to ban them from the classroom.

Let's think about cell phones' role as learning tools. Annie needs a calculator but forgot hers. She takes out her cell phone and can use the calculator app on the phone. Just across the room, Johnny is trying to spell the word "similar," so he uses the dictionary app on his phone to find the correct spelling. Mitchell, has completed all of his work early, so he decides to use the multiplication app on his phone to review multiplication facts in a fun and interactive way. These devices are causing teachers and other school officials to see that cell phones give students access to resources that actually save schools money.

While cell phones may sound great, not every school district is ready to lift the cell phone ban. There are still those that have major concerns. One concern is what to do about students who do not have a cell phone. Another worry is how to make sure students are using the phone as a learning tool instead of texting and social media. Additional concerns arise with how to address when a phone is broken or stolen while at school. Certainly, the list of problems that some schools have goes on and on.

The answer isn't clear for schools across the United States. Some schools are starting to lift the cell phone ban, but others are keeping it in place. As students pack backpacks with cell phones, the discussion of having them in the classroom will certainly continue.

Always Worked Fine Before

I hear all of this talk about allowing cell phones in the classroom. Why? There is nothing wrong with the way things are now. If you allow cell phones in our classrooms, you are asking for trouble.

Cell phones encourage students to get off task. Students may tell you that they are playing learning games, but how do you know they are not sending texts? Also, they may skip doing their assignments just so they can hurry and play these learning games. In addition, cell phones will make classrooms noisier. If everyone gets messages, plays games, or receives phone calls, think about how noisy classrooms will be.

We really do not need cell phones in our classrooms. It seems to me that the way our classrooms are right now is great. They are helping prepare me and other students for the future.

4. What is a key point difference in the two passages?

- Ⓐ Both passages think that cell phones are very bad to have at school.
- Ⓑ "Cell Phones in the Classroom" gives the positives and negatives of having cell phones at school. "Always Worked Fine Before" only tells the negatives of having cell phones at school.
- Ⓒ Both authors support the use of cell phones in the classroom.
- Ⓓ Both passages have a negative opinion of principals having the say-so of who gets to have cell phones at school.

5. What is a key similarity in the two passages?

- Ⓐ Both authors want cell phones used in the classroom as learning tools.
- Ⓑ Both passages are written by a student.
- Ⓒ Both authors dislike school and think that cell phones will make the learning experience more positive.
- Ⓓ Both authors are concerned that the use of cell phones could lead to students getting off task.

Question 6 and 7 are based on the passage below

Madison Elementary

Madison Elementary has adopted a new uniform policy for students. The students are not happy about the policy. They decided to get together to write a letter to the school board to explain their feelings about uniforms. Each grade appointed one student to present the letter as a group to the school board at their next meeting. The school board listened to the group of students and told them that they would discuss it. The board members talked over the student's concerns and decided to get rid of the new policy. The students would not have to wear uniforms after all.

Jefferson Elementary

The Jefferson Elementary school board has written a new policy about school snacks. The board decided that students would no longer be able to bring snacks from home. The school would give the students healthy snacks such as fruits and vegetables instead. The students were not pleased with the new policy. They complained to their parents, their teachers, and the principal. Their parents, teachers, and principal all were in favor of the healthy snacks. So the students at Jefferson Elementary were stuck with the healthy snacks.

6. What is a similarity between the two passages?

(A) Both passages are about a new policy on healthy snacks.
(B) Both passages are about new policies that the schools have adopted.
(C) Both policies were changed by the school board once the students expressed their dislike of the policies.
(D) There were no similarities in the two passages.

7. What is the difference between the two passages?

(A) The Madison Elementary school board changed the policy once the students talked to them about their concerns. Jefferson Elementary did not change their policy about healthy snacks after the students stated their concerns.
(B) The Madison Elementary students did not go in front of the school to state their concerns. The Jefferson Elementary students went in front of the school board.
(C) Madison Elementary policy on school uniforms was not changed but the Jefferson Elementary school policy on uniforms was changed.
(D) There were no differences noted in these passages.

Question 8 is based on the passage below

Fable A.
Once a gazelle was running as fast as she could possibly go to outrun the lion who was pursuing her. She had a good lead, and was probably going to outrun the lion, when she came to a river. Although she could swim, the water looked cold and uninviting. She hesitated on the bank of the river, not wanting to jump in. While she debated, the lion overtook her and she became his dinner.

Fable B.
Once a gazelle was running as fast as she could possibly go to outrun the lion who was pursuing her. She had a good lead, and was probably going to outrun the lion, when she came to a river. Without looking, she jumped into the water where a crocodile was waiting and she became his dinner.

8. Part A

What is a major difference in these two fables?

Ⓐ There are no differences in these fables the gazelle gets eaten in both fables.
Ⓑ The gazelle in fable A did not jump into the river and the gazelle in fable B did jumped right into the river.
Ⓒ The gazelle in fable A could not swim and the gazelle in fable B could swim.
Ⓓ The gazelle in fable A was eaten by a crocodile and the gazelle in fable B was eaten by a lion.

Part B

What is a major similarity in the two fables?

Ⓐ These two fables are not similar.
Ⓑ The gazelle in fable A and the gazelle in fable B both jumped into the river.
Ⓒ The gazelles in both fables were eaten in the end.
Ⓓ The gazelle in fable A and the gazelle in fable B were running away from a crocodile.

> **Question 9 and 10 are based on the passage below**

Picture Day

It is picture day at school and Sara is so excited. She is going to wear her new pink lace dress and shiny new black Mary Jane shoes. Sara's mom took extra time curling her hair this morning and even tied in a beautiful satin ribbon. Sara bound into the school feeling so pretty. She could hardly wait for her turn to get her picture taken.

Picture Day

Oh no! It's picture day at school. Melissa hates picture day, especially since her father lost his job. There is no money to buy a new dress, so she has to wear her sister's hand-me-downs. Melissa's mother tries to make her feel better by fixing her hair but nothing helps to change Melissa's mood. Melissa stomped into the school feeling ugly. Melissa was ready for this day to be over.

9. Which of the following answer choices describes a difference in the two passages?

Ⓐ Both girls are excited about picture day at school.
Ⓑ Sara is excited about picture day but Melissa is not excited about picture day.
Ⓒ Both girls wore new dresses for picture day.
Ⓓ The girls went to different schools.

10. What was one similarity in the two passages?

Ⓐ Both girls had shiny new black Mary Jane shoes.
Ⓑ Both girls were in bad moods when they entered school.
Ⓒ Both girls were going to have their pictures taken at school.
Ⓓ Both girls were in really good moods when they entered school.

Question 11 is based on the passage below

Tess

Eight-year-old Tess heard her parents talking about her little brother Andrew. She realized something was wrong. Andrew was very sick, and they did not have enough money for his treatment. Tess heard her daddy say, "Only a miracle can save him now."

Tess went to her bedroom and retrieved a jar from its hiding place. There were a few coins in it. She counted them carefully. She then made her way to the drug store. The pharmacist there was too busy to pay her any attention. "And what do you want?" he asked, annoyed at her persistence. "Can't you see that I am talking to my brother? He is here from Chicago."

Tess persisted, "My brother's really sick …….. and I want to buy a miracle. His name is Andrew. He has something bad growing inside his head and my daddy says only a miracle can save him now. So, how much does a miracle cost?" rambled Tess.

The pharmacist's brother, a well-dressed man, stooped down and asked the girl. "What kind of miracle does your brother need?" "Don't know," replied Tess, eyes welling up with tears. "I just know Mommy says he needs an operation. But my daddy can't pay for it. So, I want to use my money."

The man from Chicago asked, "How much money do you have?" "One dollar and 11 cents," said Tess. "Well, what a coincidence," smiled the man. "A dollar and 11 cents is the exact price of a miracle for your little brother." He took her money in one hand and grasped Tess's hand in the other. "Take me to where you live. "I want to see your brother and meet your parents. Let's see if I have the kind of miracle you need."

That well-dressed man was Carlton Armstrong, a neurosurgeon. He operated upon Andrew without charging any money. It wasn't long until Andrew was home and well again. "I wonder how much the surgery cost?" said Mother.

Tess smiled to herself. She knew exactly how much the miracle cost- one dollar and 11 cents….plus the immense faith of a little child.

Devon

Devon was a 3rd grader at Lincoln Elementary School. Devon had a younger sister, Heather. One day when Devon came home from school he overheard his parents talking. Devon's mother was crying. She said, "I don't know what we are going to do. We don't have that kind of money," she continued. Devon's father had his head in his hands and said nothing.

Devon spoke up and asked what was wrong. Devon's mother said, "Your sister is very ill and we don't have the money for her medication."

"How much does the medicine cost?" asked Devon.

Devon's father muttered, "It cost one hundred fifty dollars for one month supply."

Devon went to his room to think about the situation. He decided that he was going to try and raise the money for the medication. Devon got up the next morning and went door to door in his neighborhood. He asked the neighbors for a donation for his sister's medication. Devon stayed out all day trying to get enough money to help his sister. Just before dark he returned home and went straight to his room. He laid the money out on his bed and began counting. As he counted he began to cry, there was not only enough money for a month supply of medication but there was enough money for three months. Devon ran to his parents' room with the good news. Both his parents threw their arms around him to thank him for his good deed. His sister would get the help she needed.

11. **What is a key difference between the two passages? Circle the correct answer choice**

   Ⓐ Devon went out and asked for donations for his sister's medication. Tess found a doctor that would perform the surgery on her brother.
   Ⓑ Devon did nothing to try and help his sick sister and Tess did everything to try and help her brother.
   Ⓒ There were no differences in these passages.
   Ⓓ Tess raised the money through donations to help her brother and Devon found a doctor that gave him free medication for his sister.

End of Reading Informational Text

Chapter 3 - Language

Lesson 1: People, Places and Things

1. What is the plural form of the word baby?

- Ⓐ babys
- Ⓑ babies
- Ⓒ babes
- Ⓓ babeys

2. What is the plural of day?

- Ⓐ days
- Ⓑ daies
- Ⓒ daes
- Ⓓ day

3. What is the plural form of butterfly?

4. How do you make tomato plural?

- Ⓐ tomato
- Ⓑ tomatoes
- Ⓒ tomatos
- Ⓓ tomati

5. Which word in this sentence is NOT a noun? Circle the correct answer choice.

Jose played soccer all day.

- Ⓐ Jose
- Ⓑ played
- Ⓒ soccer
- Ⓓ day

6. Which word from the sentence is NOT a noun?

Most of the time older dogs are the best pets for families with children to have.

- (A) older
- (B) dogs
- (C) families
- (D) children

7. Choose the possessive noun that BEST completes the following sentence.

Taking _____ pencil was not a nice thing to do.

- (A) boy's
- (B) boys
- (C) Saads
- (D) Saad's

8. Choose the noun that best completes the following sentence.

Her baby _____ are starting to fall out.

- (A) teeth
- (B) tooth
- (C) teeths
- (D) toothes

9. Choose the <u>proper noun</u> in the following sentence.

Dr. Martinez said that she would help me get an appointment for later next week.

- (A) week
- (B) Dr. Martinez
- (C) said
- (D) appointment

10. Choose the noun that BEST completes the following sentence.

The _____ are going to be late for practice again.

- (A) girl
- (B) girls
- (C) female
- (D) Yanire

11. Which of the words from this sentence is NOT a noun? Circle the correct answer choice.

All of the children were happy when their grandmother and aunt came to visit last Sunday.

Ⓐ children
Ⓑ happy
Ⓒ aunt
Ⓓ Sunday

CHAPTER 3 → Lesson 2: Replace Those Nouns

1. **A noun is a word that is the name of a person, place, animal or thing. Which word is a noun in the sentence below?**

   Charlene is the best forward on the team this season.

   (A) is
   (B) team
   (C) this
   (D) on

2. **A pronoun is a word that takes the place of a noun. What are the pronouns in the sentence below?**

   Alice helped Jim with homework, and when he gave her a gift, she loved it.

3. **When will Monica find out where _____ new school will be?**

   What pronoun best fits in the blank?

   (A) Jamie's
   (B) her
   (C) she
   (D) his

4. **Charles lost _____ puppy in the park!**

   What pronoun best fits in the blank?

   (A) her
   (B) his
   (C) himself
   (D) herself

5. My pencil fell off of my desk and _____ **broke in half.**

What pronoun best completes this sentence?

Ⓐ it
Ⓑ he
Ⓒ she
Ⓓ its

6. Babies feel safest when _____ **are close to** _____ **mothers.**

What pair of pronouns fit best in this sentence?

Ⓐ she, her
Ⓑ he, his
Ⓒ they, their
Ⓓ we, our

7. Which of the following is a pronoun found in the sentence below?

I think they are going to drive over to the campsite tomorrow.

Ⓐ think
Ⓑ they
Ⓒ drive
Ⓓ tomorrow

8. Choose the pronoun that BEST completes the following sentence.

I want _____ to come over to my house too.

Ⓐ him
Ⓑ he
Ⓒ me
Ⓓ we

9. Choose the subject that could replace the underlined pronoun in the following sentence.

I saw <u>them</u> at the store about an hour ago.

Ⓐ Ted
Ⓑ Ted and Terry
Ⓒ the boy
Ⓓ we

10. Choose the pronoun that BEST completes the following sentence.

Crying isn't going to solve _____ problem.

Ⓐ the
Ⓑ her
Ⓒ she
Ⓓ they

11. Choose the pronoun that BEST replaces the underlined phrase in the following sentence.

This math test is going to be hard!

Ⓐ They
Ⓑ It
Ⓒ Its
Ⓓ Them

12. Choose the pronoun that BEST replaces the underlined phrase in the following sentence.

Please take Amber, Billy, and Crystal with you.

Ⓐ they
Ⓑ we
Ⓒ them
Ⓓ us

13. Choose the pronoun that best completes the following sentence.

_____ brought me a bouquet of flowers last week.

Ⓐ They
Ⓑ We
Ⓒ Us
Ⓓ She and I

CHAPTER 3 → Lesson 3: Regular & Irregular Plural Nouns

1. Which of the following is a plural noun written correctly?

- Ⓐ childrens
- Ⓑ mice
- Ⓒ doctores
- Ⓓ womans

2. Which of the words in the sentence below is a plural noun?

We saw four deer in the field on our hiking trip.

- Ⓐ we
- Ⓑ four
- Ⓒ our
- Ⓓ deer

3. Which answer choice demonstrates the correct plural spelling for the word "berry"?

- Ⓐ berry
- Ⓑ berries
- Ⓒ berrys
- Ⓓ berryes

4. Which of the words in the sentence below is a plural noun?

My mom baked a dozen loaves of bread yesterday.

- Ⓐ loaves
- Ⓑ baked
- Ⓒ mom
- Ⓓ bread

5. What is the correct way to make the word "cactus" plural?

- Ⓐ cactus
- Ⓑ cactues
- Ⓒ cacti
- Ⓓ cactuss

6. Which of the following demonstrate a noun correctly written in plural form?

Ⓐ bookes
Ⓑ boats
Ⓒ birdes
Ⓓ brickes

7. Which of the following demonstrate a plural noun written <u>incorrectly</u>?

Ⓐ jellies
Ⓑ schools
Ⓒ mooses
Ⓓ apples

8. Which of the following nouns in the sentence below is written <u>incorrectly</u> as a plural noun?

They were sitting on the park bench when a bunch of acornes began to fall from the oak trees.

Ⓐ acornes
Ⓑ trees
Ⓒ they
Ⓓ bunch

9. What is the correct way to write the word "goose" as a plural?

10. Which of the following plural nouns is written <u>incorrectly</u>? Circle the correct answer choice from the options given below

Ⓐ women
Ⓑ bushs
Ⓒ teeth
Ⓓ grapes

11. Which of the following words is incorrectly transformed from the plural form to its singular form?

Ⓐ Countries = Country
Ⓑ Dwarfs = Dwarf
Ⓒ Wifes = Wife
Ⓓ Moose = Moose

CHAPTER 3 → Lesson 4: Awesome Abstract Nouns

1. Which word in the following sentence is an abstract noun?

The crime was committed on the corner of Jackson Avenue and Main Street.

(A) committed
(B) Avenue
(C) crime
(D) corner

2. Which word in the following quotation is an abstract noun?

"Beauty is in the eye of the beholder."

(A) beauty
(B) eye
(C) in
(D) the

3. Which of the following is an example of an abstract noun?

(A) dog
(B) wisdom
(C) apartment
(D) teacher

4. Which of the following is an example of an abstract noun?

(A) grandmother
(B) humor
(C) television
(D) telephone

5. What is the abstract noun found in the sentence below?

What time are you going to Jeremy's house tomorrow?

(A) going
(B) Jeremy's
(C) time
(D) house

6. Which of the following is an example of an abstract noun?

Ⓐ girl
Ⓑ tractor
Ⓒ daisy
Ⓓ freedom

7. Which of the following is an example of an abstract noun?

Ⓐ bravery
Ⓑ camera
Ⓒ New York
Ⓓ Christy

8. Which of the following is <u>not</u> an abstract noun?

Ⓐ evil
Ⓑ despair
Ⓒ happiness
Ⓓ dress

9. Which of the following is <u>not</u> an abstract noun?

Ⓐ idea
Ⓑ coffee
Ⓒ dream
Ⓓ hope

10. Which of the following is an accurate definition of an abstract noun?

Ⓐ An abstract noun is a noun that names something that you cannot see, touch, taste, smell, or hear, and it usually names some idea or concept.
Ⓑ An abstract noun names a specific person, place, thing, or idea.
Ⓒ An abstract noun is a noun that you can touch, see, taste, smell, or hear.
Ⓓ An abstract noun names a person, place, or thing but does not name an idea because it engages one of the five senses.

11. Which of the following is an example of an abstract noun in the sentence below?

The relief that I felt when I found my puppy, Bruno, was safe is unexplainable.

- (A) Found
- (B) Puppy
- (C) Relief
- (D) Bruno

12. Which of the following words is an example of an abstract noun in the sentence below?

The memories that were made on our camping trip will last a lifetime.

13. Which of the following words in the sentence below is an example of an abstract noun?

The teacher used treats as motivation to encourage her students to increase their reading levels.

CHAPTER 3 → Lesson 5: Simply Simple Verb Tenses

1. What is the past tense form of the verb "play"?

- Ⓐ plays
- Ⓑ played
- Ⓒ will play
- Ⓓ playing

2. Which verb tense is the underlined word written in the sentence below?

Jason <u>will try</u> to come to the party tomorrow.

- Ⓐ present
- Ⓑ past
- Ⓒ future

3. Which of the following verbs is an example of a <u>present tense</u> verb?

- Ⓐ speaks
- Ⓑ jumped
- Ⓒ will sing
- Ⓓ driven

4. Which of the following verbs is an example of a <u>future tense</u> verb?

- Ⓐ crying
- Ⓑ cried
- Ⓒ cries
- Ⓓ will cry

5. What verb tense is the underlined word written in the sentence below?

My mom <u>threw</u> my favorite pair of jeans away because they had holes in the knees.

- Ⓐ present
- Ⓑ past
- Ⓒ future

6. What is the <u>future tense</u> of the verb "chop"?

    Ⓐ will chop
    Ⓑ chopped
    Ⓒ chop
    Ⓓ chops

7. What is the <u>present tense</u> of the verb "sneeze"?

    Ⓐ sneezed
    Ⓑ will sneeze
    Ⓒ sneeze
    Ⓓ had sneezed

8. What is the verb tense of the underlined word written in the following sentence?

Daniel <u>shouted</u> for help because his foot was caught in a tree branch and he could not get down.

    Ⓐ present
    Ⓑ past
    Ⓒ future

9. Which of the following verbs is an example of a <u>past tense</u> verb?

    Ⓐ carry
    Ⓑ sleeping
    Ⓒ laughed
    Ⓓ will shop

10. What is the <u>present tense</u> of the verb "write"?

    Ⓐ write
    Ⓑ written
    Ⓒ wrote
    Ⓓ will write

11. What is the future tense of the underlined verb in the following sentence?

Kale has <u>gone</u> to the doctor because the school nurse thinks she may have broken her arm.

Ⓐ Going
Ⓑ Will go
Ⓒ Goes
Ⓓ Gone

12. What is the past tense of the underlined verb in the following sentence?

Mrs. James said that she <u>will bake</u> cookies for the class party on Friday.

13. What is the present tense of the underlined verb in the following sentence?

We <u>rode</u> the merry-go-round at the mall five times.

CHAPTER 3 → Lesson 6: Make It Make Sense

1. **Which sentence uses a subject and verb that agree?**

   (A) My sister always help my mother.
   (B) My sister always helping my mother.
   (C) My sister always helps my mother.
   (D) My sister always am helping my mother.

2. **Which sentence uses a subject and verb that agree?**

   (A) My neighbor and his dogs walks every day.
   (B) My neighbor and his dog walk every day.
   (C) My neighbor and his dog walking every day.
   (D) My neighbor and his dog do walks every day.

3. **What form of the underlined verb agrees with the subject in this sentence?**

   My sister and her friend <u>goes</u> to the park.

   (A) goes
   (B) going
   (C) go
   (D) goed

4. **What form of the underlined verb agrees with the subject in this sentence?**

   My brother and I <u>does</u> all the work at my house.

   (A) does
   (B) do
   (C) doing
   (D) done

5. **Which sentence uses a subject and verb that agree? Circle the correct answer choice.**

   (A) Steven and Mario walk to school together.
   (B) Steven and Mario walks to school together.
   (C) Steven and Mario walking to school together.
   (D) Steven and Mario do walk to school together.

6. Which sentence uses a subject and verb that agree? Circle the correct answer choice.

Ⓐ The bag of cookies are on the counter.
Ⓑ The bag of cookies is on the counter.
Ⓒ The bag of cookies am on the counter.
Ⓓ The bag of cookies be on the counter.

7. What form of the underlined verb agrees with the subject in this sentence?

Lexi plant flowers in the garden.

Ⓐ plant
Ⓑ plants
Ⓒ planting
Ⓓ am planting

8. What form of the underlined verb agrees with the subject in this sentence?

Brian cries when he fell off of the slide last Tuesday.

Ⓐ cries
Ⓑ crying
Ⓒ cried
Ⓓ cry

9. What form of the underlined verb agrees with the subject in this sentence?

My day beginned badly when I missed the school bus.

Ⓐ beginned
Ⓑ begins
Ⓒ began
Ⓓ beginning

10. Choose the word that BEST completes the following sentence.

Your essay _____ very well written.

Ⓐ was
Ⓑ will
Ⓒ are
Ⓓ ain't

11. **What form of the underlined verb agrees with the subject in this sentence?**

The team and every player _____ happy.

12. **Fill in the blank with the correct verb form**

Eating these foods _____ her more energy for the race.

CHAPTER 3 → Lesson 7: Tell Me More

1. Bears are so 'growly' means that _____.

- (A) bears roar
- (B) bears shout
- (C) bears growl
- (D) bears howl

2. Fill in the blanks with the correct descriptive word.

Giraffes have _____ necks.

- (A) longer
- (B) long
- (C) elongate
- (D) short

3. An adjective is a word that describes a noun or pronoun. What is the adjective in the sentence below?

The assignment was confusing, so I didn't do it.

- (A) assignment
- (B) confusing
- (C) I
- (D) do

4. An adverb is a word that describes a verb, an adjective, or another adverb. What is the adverb in the sentence below?

Joe was whistling merrily all morning.

- (A) Joe
- (B) whistling
- (C) merrily
- (D) morning

5. What are the two adverbs in this sentence?

I am really too busy to go to the party.

Ⓐ too, busy
Ⓑ really, too
Ⓒ really, busy
Ⓓ busy, party

6. Fill in the blanks with the correct descriptive word.

Ashley had to sharpen her pencil because it was _____.

Ⓐ sharpened
Ⓑ broken
Ⓒ yellow
Ⓓ old

7. Fill in the blanks with the correct descriptive word.

Strawberries are my favorite fruit. They are very _____.

Ⓐ sour
Ⓑ rotten
Ⓒ bitter
Ⓓ tasty

8. Fill in the blanks with the correct descriptive word.

Aaron knew he was in trouble when he saw the _____ look on his mother's face.

Ⓐ confused
Ⓑ happy
Ⓒ smiling
Ⓓ angry

9. Choose the adverb from the following sentence. Circle the correct answer choice.

The boys entered the room very slowly. I think they knew that they were in big trouble.

Ⓐ entered
Ⓑ slowly
Ⓒ boys
Ⓓ The

10. Choose the adjective from the following sentence.

Andy made a delicious apple pie for us last night.

- (A) Andy
- (B) made
- (C) a
- (D) delicious

11. Choose the word that is acting as an adjective in the following sentence.

My dear friends, I want to see you again soon.

12. Choose the word that is acting as an adverb in the following sentence.

Her behavior only mildly disrupted the actors.

CHAPTER 3 → Lesson 8: Subordinating and Coordinating Conjunctions

1. **Is the underlined conjunction in the sentence below an example of a coordinating or subordinating conjunction?**

   We will be going shopping today <u>rather than</u> going shopping on Saturday.

   Ⓐ coordinating
   Ⓑ subordinating

2. **What word in the following sentence is an example of a subordinating conjunction?**

   Francis was watching television until her friend Maris came over.

   Ⓐ watching
   Ⓑ was
   Ⓒ came
   Ⓓ until

3. **What is the correct definition of a coordinating conjunction?**

   Ⓐ A conjunction that links words, phrases, and clauses that have equal importance.
   Ⓑ A conjunction that introduces a coordinating clause.
   Ⓒ A conjunction that introduces a subordinating clause.
   Ⓓ A conjunction that shows the action that the subject is doing in a sentence.

4. **Which of the following words is an example of a coordinating conjunction?**

   Ⓐ whereas
   Ⓑ but
   Ⓒ since
   Ⓓ as soon as

5. **What is the coordinating conjunction in the sentence below?**

   You left your backpack in Ms. Thomas' class and you left your jacket in Mr. Carson's class.

   Ⓐ in
   Ⓑ left
   Ⓒ your
   Ⓓ and

6. Which of the following answer choices is an example of a subordinating conjunction?

Ⓐ nor
Ⓑ or
Ⓒ even if
Ⓓ yet

7. What is the correct definition of a subordinating conjunction?

Ⓐ A conjunction that introduces a coordinating clause.
Ⓑ A conjunction that introduces a subordinating clause.
Ⓒ A conjunction that links a word, phrase, or clause that have equal importance.
Ⓓ A conjunction is a word that refers back to the subject of a sentence.

8. What is the subordinating conjunction in the following sentence?

Travis will be going to Denver since his flight to Tampa was canceled.

Ⓐ going
Ⓑ was
Ⓒ will be
Ⓓ since

9. What is the coordinating conjunction in the following sentence?

I thought I was prepared for my math test yet when I got the test I didn't remember how to set the problems up correctly.

Ⓐ got
Ⓑ how
Ⓒ yet
Ⓓ when

10. What is the subordinating conjunction in the following sentence?

The children anxiously waited for the bell to ring; as soon as it rang they darted out the door.

Ⓐ as soon as
Ⓑ waited for
Ⓒ for
Ⓓ as it

11. Is the underlined conjunction in the sentence below an example of a coordinating or subordinating conjunction?

LaTonya said that she was getting a new bike <u>and</u> a new purse for her birthday.

12. What is the coordinating conjunction in the following sentence?

My mom cooked spaghetti for dinner but I really wanted lasagna.

CHAPTER 3 → Lesson 9: Mix Up Those Sentences

1. Giraffes are long-legged and meek.

What type of sentence is this?

Ⓐ Descriptive (paints a picture in the reader's mind)
Ⓑ Informative
Ⓒ Interrogative (asks a question)
Ⓓ Imperative (states a command or makes a request)

2. Sammy likes to play soccer, and he also likes to play basketball.

What type of sentence is this?

Ⓐ simple
Ⓑ compound
Ⓒ complex

3. When I eat too much candy, I get a stomach ache.

What type of sentence is this?

Ⓐ simple
Ⓑ compound
Ⓒ complex

4. Some children don't like to eat fruits and vegetables.

What type of sentence is this?

Ⓐ simple
Ⓑ compound
Ⓒ complex

5. Laura and Beth were allowed to go outside and play after they finished their homework.

What type of sentence is this?

Ⓐ simple
Ⓑ compound
Ⓒ complex

6. Jasmine and Donald are cousins.

What type of sentence is this?

Ⓐ simple
Ⓑ compound
Ⓒ complex

7. Our dogs can do many tricks when they want to.

What type of sentence is this?

Ⓐ simple
Ⓑ compound
Ⓒ complex

8. Choose the answer choice that is an example of a SIMPLE sentence.

Ⓐ The little bear likes berries.
Ⓑ Today is hot, but tomorrow will be even hotter.
Ⓒ Giraffes are herbivores; a carnivorous animal is a lion.
Ⓓ I think they are coming over, but you might want to call them just to be sure.

9. Choose the answer choice that is an example of a COMPOUND sentence.

Ⓐ Jeremiah likes fruits, but Jasmine prefers vegetables.
Ⓑ Please buy some toothpaste and shampoo.
Ⓒ I missed school last Monday, Tuesday, and Wednesday.
Ⓓ She forgot to study for the math test again; her grade is not going to be good, I am afraid.

10. Choose the answer choice that BEST combines the following simple sentences into one sentence.

I had math homework on Monday. I had a math project due on Tuesday. I had a math quiz on Wednesday.

Ⓐ I had math homework on Monday. I had a math project and quiz on Tuesday and Wednesday.
Ⓑ I had math homework on Monday, a math project due on Tuesday, and a math quiz on Wednesday.
Ⓒ I had math homework on Monday, a math project due on Tuesday a math quiz on Wednesday.
Ⓓ I had math homework, a project, and a quiz on Monday, Tuesday, and Wednesday.

11. Choose the word that BEST completes the following sentence.

The baby's bottle was missing _____ we looked through the entire car.

Ⓐ ,but
Ⓑ ,so
Ⓒ ,and
Ⓓ ,or

12. Choose the word that BEST completes the following sentence.

Alexander forgot his glasses on the counter _____ his mom was able to bring them to school for him.

Ⓐ ,and
Ⓑ ,but
Ⓒ ,so
Ⓓ ,like

CHAPTER 3 → Lesson 10: Capitalization Dedication

1. Which word needs to be capitalized in this sentence?

i called my mom to come and pick me up when i got sick at school.

2. Which sentence has correct capitalization?

Ⓐ i said, "i don't feel well, mom."
Ⓑ I said, "i don't feel well, mom."
Ⓒ I said, "I don't feel well, mom."
Ⓓ I said, "I don't feel well, Mom."

3. Which sentence has correct capitalization?

Ⓐ She said, "doctor, my child doesn't feel well."
Ⓑ She said, "Doctor, my child doesn't feel well."
Ⓒ She said, "Doctor, my Child doesn't feel well."
Ⓓ She said, "Doctor, My Child doesn't feel well."

4. Which word(s) need to be capitalized in this sentence?

i told grandma i was sorry.

Ⓐ i
Ⓑ i, grandma
Ⓒ grandma
Ⓓ i, grandma, sorry

5. Which word(s) need to be capitalized in this sentence?

dr. crane said it was just the flu.

Ⓐ dr.
Ⓑ dr., crane
Ⓒ dr., crane, flu
Ⓓ flu

6. How should this book title be written?

- (A) the lord of the rings
- (B) the Lord of the rings
- (C) The Lord of the Rings
- (D) The Lord Of The Rings

7. How should this book title be written?

- (A) the chronicles of narnia
- (B) The chronicles of narnia
- (C) The Chronicles of narnia
- (D) The Chronicles of Narnia

8. How should this book title be written?

- (A) From the mixed-up files of mrs.basil e.frankweiler
- (B) From the mixed-up files of Mrs. Basil E. Frankweiler
- (C) From the Mixed-up Files of Mrs.Basil E. Frankweiler
- (D) From The Mixed-up Files Of Mrs. Basil E. Frankweiler

9. Which word(s) need to be capitalized in this sentence?

grandma said she would call my dad.

- (A) grandma
- (B) she
- (C) dad
- (D) said

10. Read the book titles and make a tick mark in the column "Correct" or "Not Correct" as applicable.

	Correct	Not Correct
Little House on the Prairie		
A Wrinkle in Time		
The Lion King		
The Call of the Wild		

CHAPTER 3 → Lesson 11: Punctuation Education

1. Which address has correct punctuation?

Ⓐ 1345 Sycamore, Street Chicago IL 123452
Ⓑ 1345 Sycamore Street Chicago, IL 123452
Ⓒ 1345 Sycamore Street Chicago, IL, 123452
Ⓓ 1345 Sycamore, Street Chicago, IL, 123452

2. Which address has correct punctuation?

Ⓐ 8142 Brown, Avenue New York NY 14353
Ⓑ 8142 Brown, Avenue New York, NY 14353
Ⓒ 8142 Brown Avenue New York, NY 14353
Ⓓ 8142 Brown Avenue New York, NY, 14353

3. Which address has correct punctuation?

Ⓐ 800 Heartbreak Lane Las Vegas, NV 83902
Ⓑ 800 Heartbreak Lane Las Vegas, NV, 83902
Ⓒ 800 Heartbreak, Lane Las Vegas, NV 83902
Ⓓ 800 Heartbreak, Lane Las Vegas, NV, 83902

4. Which quotation is written correctly?

Ⓐ "Where, is my cookie?" asked the little girl.
Ⓑ "Where, is my cookie?," asked the little girl.
Ⓒ "Where is my cookie?" asked the little girl.
Ⓓ "Where is my cookie?" ,asked the little girl.

5. Which quotation uses commas correctly?

Ⓐ "Bring me a snack," said the bratty little boy, "or I'll bite you."
Ⓑ "Bring me a snack" said the bratty little boy, "or I'll bite you."
Ⓒ "Bring me a snack," said the bratty little boy "or I'll bite you."
Ⓓ "Bring me a snack" said the bratty little boy "or I'll bite you."

6. Which quotation uses commas correctly?

(A) "Please hand me that plate", said the waitress.
(B) "Please hand me that plate" said, the waitress.
(C) "Please hand me that plate," said the waitress.
(D) "Please hand me that plate", said, the waitress.

7. Choose the sentence that shows the dialogue punctuated CORRECTLY.

(A) What was that noise asked Jason
(B) "I think it was thunder" replied Junior
(C) "There it goes again," exclaimed Jason.
(D) "are you scared" asked Junior?

8. Choose the word that Best completes the following sentence.

The _____ report showed that her teeth were very clean.

(A) dentists
(B) dentists'
(C) dentist's
(D) dentists's

9. Choose the word that BEST completes the following sentence.

A _____ way of protecting itself is its awful smell.

(A) skunks
(B) skunks'
(C) skunk's
(D) skunk

10. Choose the word that BEST completes the following sentence.

My _____ car is going to be ready to pick up sometime tomorrow.

(A) parents'
(B) parents
(C) parent's
(D) parent

11. **Choose the punctuation mark that should be added in the space shown in the following sentence.**

    "It is only 3:00_____" replied Leon.

    Ⓐ a period (3:00.")'
    Ⓑ a quotation mark (3:00"")
    Ⓒ a comma (3:00,")
    Ⓓ a question mark (3:00?")

12. Jamie screamed, There is a spider.

    Punctuate the sentence correctly and write it in the box below.

CHAPTER 3 → Lesson 12: The Comma and Quotation Dilemma

1. Which of the following answers correctly uses a comma and quotation marks?

Ⓐ "Did you find the ball, asked Thomas "if not I will look for it too."
Ⓑ Elizabeth, shouted I hate my little brother"
Ⓒ Grant asked, "Can I have some more pizza?"
Ⓓ "She said I hope, it snows tomorrow."

2. Which of the following answers correctly uses a comma and quotation marks?

Ⓐ "Amber said," we need to go to the movies on Sunday.
Ⓑ Perry asked, "Are you going to be at the meeting tonight?"
Ⓒ "He replied," "I want a computer for my birthday."
Ⓓ "Let's visit the neighbors tomorrow instead of today suggested, Sammie."

3. Which of the following answers correctly uses a comma and quotation marks?

Ⓐ "There will be a math test tomorrow," stated Mr. Thompson.
Ⓑ "there will be a math test tomorrow stated Mr. Thompson."
Ⓒ "There will be a math test tomorrow. Stated Mr. Thompson.
Ⓓ "There will be a math test tomorrow. stated" Mr. Thompson.

4. Which of the following answers correctly uses commas and quotation marks? Choose the correct answer from the options given below by circling it.

Ⓐ Grandmother said "we are going to the zoo next week."
Ⓑ "Did you see the meteor shower last night?, asked Randy."
Ⓒ Jill, said. "I don't like this chocolate cake.
Ⓓ "Hillary was not at school this week," stated Peter.

5. **Which of the following answer choices accurately describes the correct placement of commas when used in dialogue?**

Ⓐ Place a comma after the person has spoken if the quote follows.
  Ex. Mark asked, "Is it supposed to snow?"
Ⓑ Commas are not used in dialogue. Only quotation marks and ending punctuation should be used to set off quotations.
  Ex. Edward asked. "Do you have a pencil I can borrow?"
Ⓒ Place commas at the end of the quote and at the end of the sentence.
  Ex. "I am going to cook a pizza for lunch," said Terry,
Ⓓ Always place a comma after the person's name that is speaking.
  Ex. "My favorite toy truck broke." said Tony,
  Lawanda, said. "I got a bad grade on my science test."

6. **Which of the following answer choices correctly punctuates the dialogue below?**

Walker said it is going to be a long day

Ⓐ Walker said. "it is going to be a long day.
Ⓑ Walker said, "It is going to be a long day."
Ⓒ Walker, said. "It is going to be a long day?"
Ⓓ Walker "said, it is going to be a long day."

7. **Which of the following answer choices correctly punctuates the dialogue below?**

I hope that I get that new football video game for my birthday stated Perry

Ⓐ "I hope that I get that new football video game for my birthday stated Perry."
Ⓑ I hope that I get that new football video game for my birthday, "stated Perry."
Ⓒ "I hope that I get that new football video game for my birthday," stated Perry.
Ⓓ "I hope that I get that new football video game for my birthday" stated Perry.

8. **Which of the following answer choices correctly punctuates the dialogue below?**

May I have your attention said Mrs. Williams I would like to introduce a new student to our class

Ⓐ "May I have your attention," said Mrs. Williams, "I would like to introduce a new student to our class."
Ⓑ "May I have your attention said Mrs. Williams" I would like to introduce a new student to our class."
Ⓒ "May I have your attention, said Mrs. Williams, I would like to introduce a new student to our class."
Ⓓ May I have your attention, said Mrs. Williams. "I would like to introduce a new student to our class."

9. Which of the following answer choices correctly punctuates the dialogue below?

Come into the kitchen called my mom we need to make a list of ingredients to make cookies

Ⓐ "Come into the kitchen called my mom." We need to make a list of ingredients to make cookies.

Ⓑ "Come into the kitchen," called my mom. "we need to make a list of ingredients to make cookies."

Ⓒ "Come into the kitchen," called my mom, "we need to make a list of ingredients to make cookies."

Ⓓ "Come into the kitchen, called my mom, we need to make a list of ingredients to make cookies."

10. Which of the following answer choices accurately describes why quotation marks are used in dialogue?

Ⓐ Quotation marks are not used in dialogue.

Ⓑ Quotation marks are used to identify the exact words someone has spoken.

Ⓒ Quotation marks are only used to identify what a person said if they are asking a question.

Ⓓ Quotation marks are only used to identify what a person said if they are giving a command.

11. Which of the following answers correctly uses commas and quotation marks?
   Choose the correct answer from the options given below by circling it.

Ⓐ "Bring me your papers said Mr. Golf, I need to grade them."

Ⓑ "Bring me your papers, said Mr. Golf I need to grade them."

Ⓒ "Bring me your papers said Mr. Golf I need to grade them."

Ⓓ "Bring me your papers," said Mr. Golf, "I need to grade them."

CHAPTER 3 → Lesson 13: Same Name, Different Game

Question 1 and 2 are based on the poem below

Camels are bumpy,
Their backs are all lumpy,
Giraffes are long- legged and meek:
Bears are so growly,
Hyenas are holy,
Dolphins are slippery and sleek.

Kangaroos have a pocket,
But no way to lock it,
Their babies can look out and peep,
But monkeys are funny
I wish I had money,
Enough to buy one and keep.

1. **What's a kangaroo's pocket called in this poem?**

   Ⓐ a purse
   Ⓑ a pouch
   Ⓒ a packet
   Ⓓ a parcel

2. **Patterns in nature are not just pretty adornments. They do serve a purpose that has helped nature survive and flourish.**

   What does *survive* mean as it is used in this sentence?

   Ⓐ Die
   Ⓑ Go away
   Ⓒ Stay alive
   Ⓓ Perish

The ostrich is the largest bird in the world, but it cannot fly. Its legs are so strong and long that it can travel faster by running. Ostriches use their wings to help them gather speed when they start to run. They also use them as brakes in turning and stopping.

Ostriches have been known to run at speeds of 96 kms per hour. So, they can run faster than horses and match the average speed of car drivers on a highway.

These huge birds stand as tall as horses and sometimes weigh as much as 135 pounds. In North Africa, they are often seen with other larger animals. The zebra, which is also a fast runner, seems to be one of their favorite companions.

Each ostrich egg weighs as much as two dozen chicken eggs, or one and a half kg. Ostrich eggs are delicious and are often used for food by people in Africa. The shells also are made into cups and ornaments.

3. What does ornaments mean as it is used in this paragraph?

Ⓐ Statues
Ⓑ Jewelry
Ⓒ Books
Ⓓ Caps

4. What does this sentence mean?
The Constitution guarantees that a citizen has the right to freedom of speech.

Ⓐ A citizen has the right to express their thoughts and opinions.
Ⓑ A citizen has the right to wear any clothing of their choice.
Ⓒ A citizen must have the ability to communicate effectively.
Ⓓ A citizen has the right to publish and distribute their own written works.

5. What does this sentence mean?
Betty bought a new dress for the ball.

Ⓐ Betty bought a new dress for the formal dance.
Ⓑ Betty bought a new dress to play ball.
Ⓒ Betty bought a new dress to go shopping for a new ball.
Ⓓ Betty tore her dress playing ball, so she had to buy a new one.

6. **What is the meaning of this sentence?**
   The robber buried his money in the bank.

   Ⓐ The robber buried his money in the financial office.
   Ⓑ The robber buried his money beside the river.
   Ⓒ The robber felt guilty, so he took his money back to the bank.
   Ⓓ The robber dug a hole underneath the bank, where he placed his money.

7. **What does *batter* mean as it is used in this sentence?**
   The batter was too thick.

   Circle the correct answer choice from the list given below

   Ⓐ mixture used for cakes
   Ⓑ a baseball player who was up to bat
   Ⓒ the baker that was trying to learn to play baseball
   Ⓓ someone who bakes cakes

8. **What does *bill* mean as it is used in this sentence?**
   The bill was very expensive.

   Ⓐ a duck's beak
   Ⓑ money owed
   Ⓒ the man
   Ⓓ money

9. **What does *die* mean as it is used in this sentence?**
   We can't continue the game until we find the die.

   Ⓐ One of the dice
   Ⓑ No longer living
   Ⓒ A chemical used for changing the color of an item
   Ⓓ A player

10. **What is the meaning of this sentence?**
    We have to find a fair way to divide the cookies.

    Ⓐ We have to divide the cookies the way they do at the fair.
    Ⓑ We have to divide the cookies equally.
    Ⓒ These cookies must be created the same way they are at the fair.
    Ⓓ One person is going to receive more cookies than the others.

11. What prefix should be added to the word "game" to mean before the game?

12. What prefix should be added to the word "tell" to show that the student told the story again?

CHAPTER 3 → Lesson 14: Context Clue Crew

1. Which word means "time of day after the morning, but before the night"?

- (A) afternoon
- (B) noonafter
- (C) aftermoon
- (D) dawn

Amy, Ingrid, and Rebecca were friends. They went to school together. They had to cross a river on the way to school. The only way that they could cross it was by walking on a narrow tree trunk.

2. In the above paragraph, what is the meaning of the word "narrow"?
Circle the correct answer choice from among the options given below.

- (A) the size of a bus
- (B) very large
- (C) not so wide
- (D) the size of a car

Amy and her friends were off to school as usual. As they were crossing the narrow bridge, Rebecca, who was right in the back of the line, slipped on the narrow bridge. She gave a frightened scream, clutching hold of Ingrid who was in front of her. Both of them lost their balance and fell into the river. Amy clutched her mother in fright. For a moment, she hesitated and then threw herself into the river after her friends, determined to save them.

3. Which of the following words have the same meaning as "frightened"?

- (A) afraid
- (B) brave
- (C) strong
- (D) timid

The pharmacist's brother, a well-dressed man, stooped down and asked the girl about her brother.

4. What does "stooped" mean in this sentence?

Ⓐ flew
Ⓑ sat
Ⓒ bent
Ⓓ lay

5. When you "annoy" a person, that person _____ .

Ⓐ is thankful.
Ⓑ is irritated.
Ⓒ is happy.
Ⓓ is friendly.

When the judge asked the woman to explain why she didn't pay the doctor, the woman said, "Sir, before the operation, I was partially blind, but at least I could see the things in my room."

6. What is the meaning of the word "partially" according to the above sentence?

Ⓐ partly
Ⓑ completely
Ⓒ not so clear
Ⓓ clearly

Once upon a time there was a wealthy woman that could not see clearly. She called a doctor to treat her and restore her eyesight.

7. What does the phrase "restore her eyesight" mean?

Ⓐ Make her completely blind.
Ⓑ Make her able to see well again.
Ⓒ Make her able to see objects that are near.
Ⓓ Make her able to see objects that are far.

Kamil's mom told him that he had <u>bitten off more than he could chew</u>.

8. What does the underlined phrase in this sentence most likely mean?

- (A) He had taken too big of a bite.
- (B) He was wasting his time.
- (C) He had taken on too many new responsibilities.
- (D) He is not eaten enough.

(1) Andy wants to learn how to ride his bike. (2) His dad tried to teach him on Monday, but Andy was inattentive. (3) His dad tried to teach him on Tuesday, but he was inattentive. (4) His dad tried to teach him on Wednesday, but he was inattentive. (5) Andy's inattentiveness happened over and over again. (6) Now, when he tries to go down the hills, he <u>accelerates</u> too fast, which leaves him frightened. (7) When his dad returns from work, he is going to try to <u>persuade</u> him to show him the basics of riding a bike. (8) This time, he plans to follow his dad's instructions, instead of not listening carefully.

9. What does the underlined word in sentence 6 (accelerates) MOST LIKELY mean?

- (A) speeds up
- (B) slows down
- (C) stops
- (D) wrecks

10. What does the underlined word in sentence 7 (persuade) MOST LIKELY mean?

- (A) make him
- (B) convince
- (C) violently force
- (D) ignore

[1]Maria is a very intelligent third-grade student at Sunshine Elementary. [2]She is a <u>diligent</u> worker that wants to make straight A's. [3]Last night; she had a plethora of homework that took her several hours to finish. [4]She had two pages of math homework to complete. [5]She had a spelling worksheet. [6]She had a page of science homework. [7]She had one page of social studies homework to complete. [8]Her parents understand that she attends one of the top schools in the state and this requires a lot of hard work. [9]However, they feel that this amount of work is a bit absurd. [10]There is no time for their daughter's extracurricular activities. [11]They are going to call the school later today to discuss their concerns.

11. What does the underlined word in sentence 2 (diligent) MOST LIKELY mean?
   Write your answer in the box given below.

CHAPTER 3 → Lesson 15: The Root and Affix Institute

1. What is the prefix in the word *bewailed*?

- (A) be-
- (B) bew-
- (C) -ed
- (D) wail

2. What is a *telescope*?

- (A) An instrument that helps us to see small objects by making them look bigger
- (B) An instrument that helps us to get a closer view of objects far away
- (C) An instrument that helps us to measure speed of a vehicle
- (D) An instrument that helps us to keep things cold and preserve them

3. Which part of the word *treatment* is a suffix?

- (A) -ment
- (B) treat-
- (C) trea-
- (D) -atment

4. In the word *coincidence*, 'co-' is the _____.

- (A) suffix
- (B) root word
- (C) prefix
- (D) helping word

5. How many legs does a tripod have?

- (A) one
- (B) two
- (C) three
- (D) four

6. Look at the following pairs of words.

    happy - unhappy

    cover - uncover

    lock - unlock

    When the prefix 'un' is added to the word, what happens to its meaning?

    Ⓐ The meaning remains the same.

    Ⓑ The meaning becomes opposite of the given word.

    Ⓒ The word becomes a synonym of the given word.

    Ⓓ The word becomes clear to understand.

7. Based on the following sentences, what does the prefix "anti-," mean?

    The abolitionists were <u>antislavery</u>.

    The peace marchers are <u>antiwar</u>.

    He doesn't like to go to parties; he is <u>antisocial</u>.

    Ⓐ in favor of

    Ⓑ against

    Ⓒ before

    Ⓓ after

8. Based on the following sentences, what does the prefix "micro," mean?

    A <u>microchip</u>, a tiny part of an electronic or computer device.

    A <u>microscope</u> looks at tiny creatures.

    A <u>microphone</u> makes a soft sound louder.

    Ⓐ creature

    Ⓑ larger

    Ⓒ loud

    Ⓓ small

9. Based on the following sentences, what does the prefix "tele-," mean?

    A <u>telescope</u> is used to look at distant things.

    A <u>telephone</u> is used to place long distance calls.

    A <u>television</u> receives a signal from far away.

    Ⓐ again

    Ⓑ distant

    Ⓒ nearby

    Ⓓ short

10. Based on the following sentences, what does the prefix "un-," mean?
   The heavy jacket is <u>uncomfortable</u> in hot weather.
   Karla was <u>unhappy</u> when her dog died.
   He couldn't tell which answer was right; he felt <u>uncertain</u>.

   Ⓐ comfortable
   Ⓑ very
   Ⓒ not
   Ⓓ sure

11. Match the word to its Prefix.

   Write the prefix to match the word in the blank boxes.

Disagree	
Prearrange	
Abnormal	

12. Write the Prefix, Root word and Suffix in the correct order for the word "Disagreeable" in the boxes given below.

   Prefix   **Root Word**   **Suffix**

CHAPTER 3 → Lesson 16: Making Words Work

1. Which list of words rhyme?

- Ⓐ toil, boil, soil
- Ⓑ soil, bail, tail
- Ⓒ twin, win, swing
- Ⓓ song, hung, sung

2. What word is a synonym for anxiously? Choose the correct word and circle it.

Maria waited anxiously for the concert to begin.

- Ⓐ unfriendly
- Ⓑ uneasily
- Ⓒ easily
- Ⓓ happily

3. What word is an antonym for the bold word in the sentence?

He couldn't believe his luck. "Ha! Ha!" he **laughed**.

- Ⓐ happy
- Ⓑ unhappy
- Ⓒ cried
- Ⓓ giggled

4. Which set of words rhymes with "brought"?

- Ⓐ bought, bring
- Ⓑ thought, sought
- Ⓒ bringing, buy, bring
- Ⓓ None of the above

5. What is a homophone for "there"?

- Ⓐ them
- Ⓑ their
- Ⓒ those
- Ⓓ this

6. Which word is a synonym for "quarreled"?

Kelsey and Maya quarreled again. They both wanted to play with the soccer ball.

- (A) discussed
- (B) yelled
- (C) fought
- (D) fit

7. What is the antonym of "night"?

- (A) dark
- (B) light
- (C) sleep
- (D) morning

8. What list of words contains antonyms for the word "wrong"?

- (A) right, correct
- (B) wrong, strong
- (C) amazed, right
- (D) write, right

9. Which list of words contains rhyming words?

- (A) brother, another, strong
- (B) along, wrong, right
- (C) black, brother, back
- (D) slight, right, night

10. What is an antonym of the word "deep"?

- (A) profound
- (B) shallow
- (C) meaningful
- (D) secret

11. Which word means the opposite of *whisper*? Circle the correct answer choice.

- (A) talk
- (B) look
- (C) quiet
- (D) scream

12. What is the antonym of the word "Carefully"? Write your answer in the box below.

CHAPTER 3 → Lesson 17: Connecting Related Words

1. Which of the following sentences has the same meaning as the sentence below?

The principal was infuriated that someone had pulled the fire alarm.

Ⓐ The principal was calm when someone pulled the fire alarm.
Ⓑ The principal was relaxed when someone pulled the fire alarm.
Ⓒ The principal was enraged that someone had pulled the fire alarm.
Ⓓ The principal was excited that someone had pulled the fire alarm.

2. Read the below list of words:
   A. Enormous
   B. Slight
   C. Minute
   D. Average

There were a tremendous number of people at the concert last night.

Which word is similar to the underlined word in the above sentence? Write the correct answer in the box given below.

3. Which word is most extreme in its meaning?

Ⓐ cheerful
Ⓑ happy
Ⓒ delighted
Ⓓ overjoyed

4. Which answer choice is similar to "whisper"?

Ⓐ screech
Ⓑ chatter
Ⓒ murmur
Ⓓ scream

5. Which of the following sentences has the same meaning as the sentence below?

During the scavenger hunt our team had a hard time finding a sphere.

- Ⓐ During the scavenger hunt our team had a hard time finding a cone.
- Ⓑ During the scavenger hunt our team had a hard time finding an orb.
- Ⓒ During the scavenger hunt our team had a hard time finding a cylinder.
- Ⓓ During the scavenger hunt our team had a hard time finding a cube.

6. Which of the answer choices has a similar meaning as "slippery"?

- Ⓐ dry
- Ⓑ slick
- Ⓒ tacky
- Ⓓ rough

7. Which of the following words is the least extreme in its meaning?

- Ⓐ enemy
- Ⓑ attacker
- Ⓒ rival
- Ⓓ competitor

8. Which of the following sentences does NOT have the same meaning as the sentence below?

Lily froze in her tracks when she saw the large scary dog approaching.

- Ⓐ Lily halted in her tracks when she saw the large terrifying dog approaching.
- Ⓑ Lily stopped in her tracks when she saw the large dangerous looking dog approaching.
- Ⓒ Lily darted when she saw the large frightening dog approaching.
- Ⓓ Lily stopped in her tracks when she saw the large horrifying dog approaching.

9. Which of the following answer choices has a similar meaning to the word "possible"?

- Ⓐ potential
- Ⓑ impossible
- Ⓒ unlikely
- Ⓓ unattainable

10. Which of the following answer choices is least like the word "naughty"?

- Ⓐ rowdy
- Ⓑ behaved
- Ⓒ evil
- Ⓓ unruly

CHAPTER 3 → Lesson 18: Vocabulary Acquisition

1. **Which of the following domain specific words means "the number below the line in a fraction and tells how many equal parts there are in the whole"? Circle the correct answer choice**

   Ⓐ fragment
   Ⓑ denominator
   Ⓒ reproduction
   Ⓓ difference

2. **In which class would you most likely talk about "mammals"?**

   Ⓐ Math
   Ⓑ Social Studies
   Ⓒ English Language Arts
   Ⓓ Science

3. **If your teacher asked you to list a "sequence of events" from a story that you just read, what is she asking you to do?**

   Ⓐ The teacher wants you to put the events in order as they occurred in the story.
   Ⓑ The teacher wants you to summarize the story in your own words.
   Ⓒ The teacher wants you to list the main idea and the supporting points from the story.
   Ⓓ The teacher wants you to write your own story that has a similar plot as the story you read.

4. **In which class would you most likely hear the domain-specific word "hyperbole"?**

   Ⓐ Math
   Ⓑ Science
   Ⓒ Social Studies
   Ⓓ English Language Arts

5. **If your teacher asked you to "estimate" the amount of time you spent studying for the spelling test, what is he asking you to do?**

   Ⓐ The teacher wants you to write a detailed report of your study habits.
   Ⓑ The teacher wants you to give an approximate amount of time that you have spent studying.
   Ⓒ The teacher wants an exact amount of time you spent studying.
   Ⓓ The teacher wants you to write your spelling words down and study them.

6. **If the directions of an assignment require you to provide "evidence" to support your short answer responses, what information are you being asked to provide?**

   Ⓐ The directions are asking you to write your opinion of what you think is the correct answer to the question.
   Ⓑ The directions want you to show the sources that support the answer responses.
   Ⓒ The directions want you to give the answer that you think is correct.
   Ⓓ The directions want you to find the key points of the chapter you are studying.

7. **Mrs. Johnson's science class is studying "moon phases". Which of the following is an accurate definition of "moon phases"?**

   Ⓐ Moon phases- the path that the moon follows as it rotates around the planets.
   Ⓑ Moon phases- a chart that tells you when the moon will rise every day.
   Ⓒ Moon phases- the appearance of the lit portion of the moon as seen by an observer.
   Ⓓ Moon phases- the type of weather the Earth will be experiencing with the moon.

8. **What does the academic word "maximum" mean?**

   Ⓐ The smallest amount required
   Ⓑ The average number that needs to be provided
   Ⓒ The range of numbers that is required
   Ⓓ The largest number of items that can be provided

9. **In which class would you most likely learn about "subordinating conjunctions"?**

   Ⓐ Social Studies
   Ⓑ English Language Arts
   Ⓒ Math
   Ⓓ Science

Mr. Nelson separated his class into groups. There were four in each group. Each member of the group was assigned to write a "verse" of a poem about the seasons.

10. **What will each student have to write?**

   Ⓐ Each student will to write one line for the group's poem.
   Ⓑ Each student will write four lines for the group's poem.
   Ⓒ Each student will write a separate poem and edit each other's work.
   Ⓓ Each student will to write a single word for the group's poem.

11. If your teacher wants you to "justify" your answer, what is your teacher asking you to do?

1. Contractions are made by joining two words into one word and leaving out a letter. You put an ' in place of the missing letter to make the contraction. Some kinds of contractions combine a word with the word "are". The letter "a" is then left out and the 'put in. Some kinds combine a word with the word "is". The letter "i" is left out and the ' put in. Read the first word and second word in each row and write contractions in the contraction column

First word	Second word	contraction
they	are	
we	are	
she	is	
he	is	
you	are	

2. Which 2 sentences have contractions in them? Mark them.

   Ⓐ Jamie and I played in the park with our friends.
   Ⓑ We aren't going to go shopping until Friday.
   Ⓒ They're happy to go on vacation.
   Ⓓ She ran home for supper.

3. Write the contractions with the words below using not as the second word. Remember to leave out the "o" in not and add an '.

   a. are = _____

   b. have = _____

   c. did = _____

   d. is = _____

4. There are a couple of words that change completely when not is added as the second word and a contraction is made. Will not becomes won't and cannot becomes can't. Pick the sentence below that has one of these contractions in it. Mark your answer.

Ⓐ Latifa can go into town with us.
Ⓑ The cows will eat their hay when it gets cold.
Ⓒ The firemen won't let the fire spread.
Ⓓ The police helped the lady cross the street.

5. Read the sentences and choose the right contraction to put in each blank.

a. They _____ sad anymore because they found their puppy. (aren't, can't)

b. The movie _____ going to start for one hour. (didn't, isn't)

c. _____ play video games after we do our homework. (Let's, You've)

d. She said _____ tried to make it before and failed. (I'm, she'd)

6. When talking about something that belongs to someone, we call it possessive. If you are talking about a thing that belongs to someone, add an 's at the end of the person's or animal's name. If the word already ends in an "s" only add the '.

Make the nouns possessive.

Nouns	Possessive
Manuel	
Tony	
Bess	
Emanuel	
Mr. Brown	
Ms. Bliss	

7. **Which of the following groups of words do NOT show possession? Mark them.**

   Ⓐ Large dresses
   Ⓑ Bonnie's friends
   Ⓒ Natasha's pets
   Ⓓ Fancy hats
   Ⓔ Spicy cheeseburgers
   Ⓕ Matilda's house

8. **Read the sentences and mark 2 that use possessive nouns correctly.**

   Ⓐ Mr. Langleys class had a party today.
   Ⓑ My sister's room is a mess!
   Ⓒ He listens to Brad's music all the time.
   Ⓓ Why did Todds dad get a job in another town?

9. **Unscramble the words to make a sentence using the possessive noun correctly.**

   mother her keep let Patty's the tiny kitten.

   | |
   | |
   | |

10. **Find the 4 possessives in the story and highlight them. One may be seen 2 times. Be sure to highlight all 4.**

    Mary's best friend was Vicky. Vicky's mom let them go to the park. The girls had fun. On the way home, they stopped at Vicky's favorite ice cream parlor. Beth and Susan were there, too. The girls' laughter was heard all over the store.

1. Remember that holidays are always capitalized. Read the list of words and mark the holidays.

   Ⓐ Easter
   Ⓑ Eggs
   Ⓒ Memorial Day
   Ⓓ Valentine's Day
   Ⓔ Presents

2. Read the sentences below. Mark the one that uses capitalization correctly for holidays.

   Ⓐ The family went on a vacation for the fourth of July.
   Ⓑ Mary and her mother made cupcakes for Veteran's Day.
   Ⓒ The team rode in a parade on president's day.
   Ⓓ Grandpa does not like halloween.

3. Names of products are capitalized, too. Examples of these are Cheerios for a cereal, and Kraft for cheese or milk products. If an exact name is not there, do not capitalize it. Read the words in the box and mark if they should be capitalized.

	Capitalize	Do not capitalize
Ford		
Truck		
Amazon		
Dog food		
M & M's		
Candy		
Store		
Coca Cola		

4. **Read the sentences below. Mark the 2 that use product names correctly.**

Ⓐ Most people like to eat Lay's chips.
Ⓑ He drove a bright shiny Toyota truck.
Ⓒ The dentist says to use crest toothpaste.
Ⓓ We feed our dog purina dog chow.

5. **Fix the sentence below using the product names. Remember to capitalize the product name. Write it correctly.**

   His brother drove a chevrolet 4x4 truck, but his mom liked her buick car better.

6. **Names of places must be capitalized, too. Countries, states, cities, landmarks, highways, and streets are examples of these. Read the words below. Make them capitalized.**

   a. main street _____

   b. dallas, texas _____

   c. japan _____

   d. yellowstone national park _____

7. **Read the sentences and underline the words that are names of places.**

   Rolando says Hawaii is the best place to go on a vacation.

   Many people go to Washington Avenue to shop.

   I have never visited England, but I want to go there one day.

   My favorite store is Target.

8. Read the list of words below. Decide if they are names of places that need to be capi talized. Rewrite and capitalize the ones that are names of places. If there are 2 or more words, be sure to capitalize all of those that need to be.

big highway

tiny store

walmart

sears

disneyworld

chicago, illinois

9. Which of the following sentences does NOT have the correct use of capitalization of names of places.

Ⓐ Howard and Samantha took a trip to South America.
Ⓑ The best chicken nuggets are at McDonald's!
Ⓒ The train stopped in biloxi, mississippi.
Ⓓ We had fun at Six Flags!

10. Write the capitalized name of a place in a sentence.

San Francisco, California.

CHAPTER 3 → Lesson 21: Conjunctions and Interjections

(1) Mary went to visit her grandmother last weekend. (2) She likes to visit her grandmother frequently. (3) While visiting, they enjoy walking. (4) They strolled in the beautiful park and talked. (5) Mary and her grandmother enjoyed their visit.

1. Which sentences contain a conjunction?

- Ⓐ sentences 1 and 2
- Ⓑ sentences 2 and 3
- Ⓒ sentences 3 and 4
- Ⓓ sentences 4 and 5

2. Identify the conjunction in the below sentence.

Billy does not like to play basketball, nor does he enjoy watching it on TV.

- Ⓐ not
- Ⓑ nor
- Ⓒ does
- Ⓓ to

3. Identify the subordinating conjunction in the below sentence.

As soon as I finish my homework, I am going to watch my favorite TV show.

- Ⓐ soon
- Ⓑ as soon as
- Ⓒ to
- Ⓓ to watch

4. Identify the <u>coordinating conjunction</u> in the below sentence.

Zelda and her family visited the Jackson Zoo last weekend although it was cold and rainy.

- Ⓐ last
- Ⓑ although
- Ⓒ and
- Ⓓ cold

5. Identify the <u>subordinating conjunction</u> in the above sentence.

Zelda and her family visited the Jackson Zoo last weekend although it was cold and rainy.

Ⓐ last
Ⓑ although
Ⓒ and
Ⓓ cold

6. Choose the compound sentence that uses the proper coordinating conjunction.

Ⓐ My favorite food is pizza, or Jenny's favorite food is tacos.
Ⓑ The junior high baseball game was exciting, nor the varsity game was even better.
Ⓒ I forgot to do my math homework, but I am being sent to detention.
Ⓓ I love horseback riding, so I am looking forward to the trail ride this weekend.

7. Identify the <u>interjection</u> in the below sentence.

No, you cannot go to the mall with your friends this weekend because we are going to visit Grandma and Grandpa.

Ⓐ no
Ⓑ to
Ⓒ because
Ⓓ and

8. Identify the <u>coordinating conjunction</u> in the below sentence.

No, you cannot go to the mall with your friends this weekend because we are going to visit Grandma and Grandpa.

Ⓐ no
Ⓑ to
Ⓒ because
Ⓓ and

9. Identify the subordinating conjunction in the below sentence.

No, you cannot go to the mall with your friends this weekend because we are going to visit Grandma and Grandpa.

Ⓐ   no
Ⓑ   to
Ⓒ   because
Ⓓ   and

10. Identify the interjection in the below sentence.

Wow! That was the most amazing trick I have ever seen.

Ⓐ   most
Ⓑ   amazing
Ⓒ   that
Ⓓ   wow

11. Go put on either your shoes and your boots.

Fix the sentence by replacing and with an appropriate conjunction.

End of Language

Notes

Additional Information

Test Taking Tips

1) **The day before the test,** make sure you get a good night's sleep.

2) **On the day of the test,** be sure to eat a good hearty breakfast! Also, be sure to arrive at school on time.

3) **During the test:**

- **Read every question carefully.**

  - Do not spend too much time on any one question. Work steadily through all questions in the section.
  - Attempt all of the questions even if you are not sure of some answers.
  - If you run into a difficult question, eliminate as many choices as you can and then pick the best one from the remaining choices. Intelligent guessing will help you increase your score.
  - Also, mark the question so that if you have extra time, you can return to it after you reach the end of the section.
  - Some questions may refer to a graph, chart, or other kind of picture. Carefully review the graphic before answering the question.
  - Be sure to include explanations for your written responses and show all work.

- **While Answering Multiple-Choice (EBSR) questions.**

  - Select the bubble corresponding to your answer choice.
  - Read **all** of the answer choices, even if think you have found the correct answer.

- **While Answering TECR questions.**

  - Read the directions of each question. Some might ask you to drag something, others to select, and still others to highlight. Follow all instructions of the question (or questions if it is in multiple parts)

Frequently Asked Questions(FAQs)

For more information on the assessment, visit
www.lumoslearning.com/a/atlas-faqs
OR Scan the **QR Code**

Why Practice with Repeated Reading Passages?

Throughout the Lumos Learning practice workbooks, students and educators will notice many passages repeat. This is done intentionally. The goal of these workbooks is to help students practice skills necessary to be successful in class and on standardized tests. One of the most critical components to that success is the ability to read and comprehend passages. To that end, reading fluency must be strengthened. According to Hasbrouck and Tindal (2006), "Helping our students become fluent readers is absolutely critical for proficient and motivated reading" (p. 642). And, Nichols et al. indicate, (2009), "fluency is a gateway to comprehension that enables students to move from being word decoders to passage comprehenders" (p. 11).

Lumos Learning recognizes there is no one-size-fits-all approach to build fluency in readers; however, the repeated reading of passages, where students read the same passages at least two or more times, is one of the most widely recognized strategies to improve fluency (Nichols et al., 2009). Repeated reading allows students the opportunity to read passages with familiar words several times until the passage becomes familiar and they no longer have to decode word by word. As students reread, the decoding barrier falls away allowing for an increase in reading comprehension.

The goal of the Lumos Learning workbooks is to increase student achievement and preparation for any standardized test. Using some passages multiple times in a book offers struggling readers an opportunity to do just that.

References

Hasbrouck, J., and Tindal, G. (2006). Oral reading fluency norms: A valuable assessment tool for reading teachers. Reading Teacher, 59(7), 636644. doi:10.1598/RT.59.7.3. Nichols, W., Rupley, W., and Rasinski, T. (2009). Fluency in learning to read for meaning: going beyond repeated readings. Literacy Research & Instruction, 48(1). doi:10.1080/19388070802161906.

Progress Chart

Standard	Lesson	Score	Date of Completion
AAS			
3.RC.1.RF 3.RC.2.RF	The Question Session		
3.RC.3.RF	Tell Me Again		
3.RC.3.RF	Caring Characters & Life Lessons		
3.RC.7.RL 3.RC.8.RL	Calling All Characters		
3.RC.7.RL 3.RC.8.RL	A Chain of Events		
3.RC.4.RF	Figurative Language Expressions		
3.RC.12.RL	Parts of a Whole		
3.RC.11.RL	Who's Talking Now?		
3.RC.5.RF 3.RC.10.RL	I Can See It Now		
3.RC.9.RL	Alike and Different		
3.RC.9.RL	Setting the Scene		
3.RC.1.RF 3.RC.2.RF	Explicitly Comprehension		
3.RC.3.RF	The Main Idea Arena		
3.RC.13.RI	Cause and Effect		
3.RC.4.RF	Educational Expressions		
3.RC.16.RI	Special Text Parts		
3.RC.18.RI	What Did You Already Know?		
3.RC.17.RI	Informational Illustrations		
3.RC.15.RI	Connect the Dots		
3.RC.14.RI	Compare and Contrast Important Points and Key Details		

Standard	Lesson	Score	Date of Completion
AAS			
3.L.4.S 3.L.5.S 3.L.6.S	People, Places, and Things		
3.L.4.S 3.L.5.S 3.L.6.S	Replace Those Nouns		
3.L.3.S	Regular & Irregular Plural Nouns		
3.L.1.S	Awesome Abstract Nouns		
3.L.10.S	Simply Simple Verb Tenses		
3.L.7.S 3.L.11.S	Make It Make Sense		
3.L.8.S 3.L.9.S 3.L.12.S	Tell Me More		
3.L.13.S	Subordinating and Coordinating Conjunctions		
3.L.17.S	Mix Up Those Sentences		
3.L.18.C	Capitalization Dedication		
3.L.22.C	Punctuation Education		
3.L.21.C	The Comma and Quotation Dilemma		
3.V.1	Same Name, Different Game		
3.V.2	Context Clue Crew		
3.V.6	The Root & Affix Institute		
3.V.5	Making Words Work		
3.V.4	Connecting Related Words		
3.V.1	Vocabulary Acquisition		
3.L.16.S	Use An Apostrophe		
3.L.20.C	How is it Capitalized?		
3.L.23.C	Conjunctions and Interjections		

Grade **3**

Lumos Learning
Step Up Your Skills

ARKANSAS
Math
ATLAS Practice

Student Copy

ONLINE

2 Practice Tests
Personalized Study Plan

Math Domains
- Number & Place Value
- Computation & Algebraic Reasoning
- Geometry & Measurement
- Data Analysis

Available
- At Leading book stores
- Online www.LumosLearning.com

Made in the USA
Columbia, SC
14 March 2024